TEXAS HIKES
—and—
BREWS

THE TEXAS EXPERIENCE

Books made possible by
Sarah '84 and Mark '77 Philpy

TEXAS Hikes and Brews

A RAMBLER'S GUIDE TO A PERFECT DAY

Jay Maddock
Debra Kellstedt

TEXAS A&M UNIVERSITY PRESS
COLLEGE STATION

First edition

♾ This paper meets the requirements of ANSI/NISO Z39.48-1992 (Permanence of Paper).
Binding materials have been chosen for durability.
Manufactured in China through Martin Book Management.

Library of Congress Cataloging-in-Publication Data

Names: Maddock, Jay E., author. | Kellstedt, Debra, 1969– author.
Title: Texas hikes and brews : a rambler's guide to a perfect day / Jay Maddock, Debra Kellstedt.
Other titles: Texas experience (Texas A & M University. Press)
Description: First edition. | College Station : Texas A&M University Press, [2025] | Series: The Texas experience | Includes bibliographical references and index.
Identifiers: LCCN 2025020496 (print) | LCCN 2025020497 (ebook) | ISBN 9781648433115 | ISBN 9781648433122 (ebook)
Subjects: LCSH: Hiking—Texas—Guidebooks. | Microbreweries—Texas—Guidebooks. | LCGFT: Guidebooks.
Classification: LCC GV199.42.T4 M33 2025 (print) | LCC GV199.42.T4 (ebook) | DDC 796.5109764—dc23/eng/20250505
LC record available at https://lccn.loc.gov/2025020496
LC ebook record available at https://lccn.loc.gov/2025020497

All photographs were taken by Debra Kellstedt except those in chapter 18 and the hiking portion of chapter 2, which were taken by Jay Maddock.

FRONTIS: Old Tree Hugger, Beer Garden Pilz, and Black Is Beautiful under the live oaks.

JM

To my boys, Jake and Josh,
who I hope can experience all of the
natural beauty we saw while writing this book.

DK

To my husband, Paul, and my daughters,
Abigail and Elizabeth, who have cheered me on
in so many of my adventures.

From both

To our friends Tom and Lou,
constant companions and great company!

★

CONTENTS

Section 2

CAPITAL CITY URBAN HIKES

Section 3

SPACE CITY AND VICINITY

Section 4

HILL COUNTRY AND OUT WEST

TEXAS HIKES and BREWS

Santa Elena Canyon, Big Bend National Park.

1

A WALK IN THE WOODS AND A COLD DRINK

Texas is famous for many things: cowboys, NASA, BBQ, Tex-Mex, belt buckles, and so much more, but to date, it has yet to be well known for its hiking. When I arrived from Hawaii in College Station, Texas, in 2015, I (Jay) asked about hiking trails. People told me, "There is Lick Creek Park." While the five-hundred-acre park is nice enough, it wasn't quite what I had in mind. After rambling for a decade and a half along many trails that cross the Hawaiian Islands, I had a high standard for hiking. Watching the emerald mountains of the Na Pali Coast greeting the undulating ocean off the coast of Kauai was hard to beat. So, I hiked Lick Creek Park several dozen times, and life got busy with work, family, and other obligations, and I sort of forgot about hiking in Texas. Then the COVID-19 pandemic hit.

As it did for many, my world turned upside down. As a public health professor, I had been waiting for a pandemic for two decades, but little did I or anyone know it would last for over a year. Living alone, I was isolated most of my week. The occasional happy hour Zoom with friends and colleagues did little to decrease my loneliness. My friend and public health colleague Debra ("Deb") Kellstedt was in Omaha, completing a postdoctoral research position at the University of Nebraska Medical Center. As the world was upended in March 2020, she returned to College Station, where her husband, Paul, and primary

Trail warning sign at Lost Maples State Natural Area.

residence were based. As physical activity researchers, we met each week during the spring and summer of 2020 to take long walks and talk about research, the pandemic, and life in general. After several months, the scenery on our paved neighborhood route started to get old, and the intense August heat shortened our walks. One day, I told Deb I was thinking about starting a hiking club where I would pick a different trail to hike each weekend with whomever wanted to go. Deb loved the idea and told me that when she ran marathons, the thing that got her through her races was always finding a local establishment where she could get a cheeseburger after the race. As we thought about our reward for hiking, the idea was straightforward: beer! Texas has a burgeoning craft beer scene, and many local microbreweries have minimal distribution outside their taprooms. This would make finding and getting a beer at these places a true treat.

Not wasting time, we headed out the following weekend, right in the middle of the August heat, on our first hike. After completing a couple of hikes and trying nearby breweries, we talked about how we were both jotting down notes about the places we went. Since we both like to write, notes became sentences, paragraphs, and then pages. We thought that the combined ramblings of two friends might make an interesting book, and luckily, Texas A&M University Press agreed, so here we are.

Did you know?

TIPS FOR A PERFECT DAY

We used the AllTrails app (alltrails.com) to find many hikes. This app has great user reviews of different hikes, suggests the best months to use the trails, and links with directions directly to the trailhead. We found it invaluable on our journeys. There are several other apps available, so take a look and choose one to help guide you.

Texas is hot most of the year. Bring plenty of water, especially if you take an unexpected detour or get lost. General recommendations are to bring half a liter (sixteen ounces or a proper pint) per hour of hiking. Given the heat in Texas, we recommend carrying a full liter for every hour you are out. You might not need it, but if you do, you will be glad you have it. I wear a CamelBak and swear by it. Deb came around and got one after about five hikes.

Trail shoes can be a good idea. Sneakers lack traction and can lead to slips and falls, especially if the trail is wet. Hiking boots can be heavy and are a bit of overkill for a day hike. Trail shoes have great traction and strong soles, so you won't get impaled by any sharp object you step on.

Bathrooms are not everywhere. If you are going to a state park, the facilities are well maintained. Many state

(*continued*)

and national forests don't have any facilities. We hit a local gas station right before approaching the trailhead.

Preparing for the elements is important, too. We recommend wearing a broad-brimmed hat on sunny days. It keeps the sun off your head, cools you down, and helps avoid sunburn. Given the sun and the bugs, we used sunscreen and bug spray before every hike. We would suggest that you do, too.

Always let someone know where you are hiking; at least one person should carry a mobile phone. This is especially true for large wilderness areas like Sam Houston National Forest, where you can be miles away from anybody else.

Use the buddy system; go with a friend or two. We enjoyed the social side of hiking just as much as nature. Outside of small, heavily trafficked green spaces, this is wise for safety, too.

Don't forget to plan to find a place for beer and food. It's what makes the perfect day!

Our well-traveled hiking shoes.

Pine Canyon Trail in Big Bend National Park.

This is not a scientific treatise or your typical guidebook. We hiked every inch of every trail described and drank every drop of beer we ordered. Our goal is to share our adventures in hopes that others will follow our path and even strike out on their own to find great places. You will notice that there are no trail maps in this book. All the state parks provide outstanding maps. For other hikes, apps like AllTrails are helpful and keep you from getting lost. We planned most of our hikes with a brewery nearby so that both can be visited in a day—and most can be done as a day trip from College Station. If you are heading out from Aggieland, a helpful appendix in the back gives you the number of miles to each location in the book. Depending on the hike, the destinations are also not too far from Houston, Austin, or Waco. Our hikes stretched from Sea Rim State Park, almost on the border of Louisiana, to Big Bend Ranch State Park, way out in West Texas (787 miles apart if you're interested).

Interestingly, we didn't go too far north or south, with most hikes falling between the latitudes of Waco and San Antonio. While most hikes tend to be stable, things can change over time. The state parks will list when a particular trail is closed for maintenance or other conditions.

For the breweries, we purposely picked smaller places that were not owned by big beverage companies. Sure, we could have visited Shiner, Saint Arnold, and Karbach, but most Texans know these beers well from their ubiquitous presence at every H-E-B store in the state. We wanted to find the cool places you've never heard of and might want to try. While some breweries were in industrial settings, most had beautiful indoor and outdoor spaces for relaxing and talking, and many provided food from a local restaurant, food truck, or their own kitchen. Breweries can and do change their offerings frequently. What we ate and drank was current at the time of writing.

Did you know?

CRAFT BEER

According to the Brewers Association, craft beer is small and independent. Even though craft beer breweries make up over 95 percent of the breweries in the United States, they account for less than a quarter of beer sales.

We have also updated all information as of summer 2024. We recommend checking specific websites before setting out on your adventure. Deb and I are on the north side of age forty but exercise regularly and are reasonably fit. We included a range of hikes in the book, from simple flat trails to full-day adventures in Big Bend. If you haven't been hiking in a while, we recommend starting with the shorter trails and working up to more challenging endeavors.

ORGANIZATION OF THE BOOK

This book is organized by geography. The first section features hikes within an hour or so of Aggieland. The second section features many hikes close to and even in Austin. The third is focused mainly on the greater Houston area. The last section is breathtaking; it starts in the Hill County and goes west. This means you don't need to read the book cover to cover. For most of the hikes, we went only once (for now). A few we visited a second time because there was still so much to see. The time of year can significantly affect your hiking experience. We often chose to hike trails in the "off-season." For example, we visited the Lost Maples State Natural Area in the winter rather than the fall. Depending on when you hike these trails, your experience could be quite different. The same could be said of the breweries. Many offer seasonal choices, from big winter stouts to refreshing summer farmhouse saisons. For the most part, we kept ourselves to two beers each per brewery and chose beer styles we liked. Our goal was not to be exhaustive but to have what we enjoyed. Most breweries will give you a sample if you ask, which is a great way to help you decide. We are the first to admit that we are not beer experts, and the brewery and beer portions of each chapter are intended chiefly to describe our overall experiences rather than provide detailed critiques of every beer on tap. If I had to tell you about my beer profile, it would be "the hoppier, the better." Deb usually leaned toward a more mellow German-style beer. But sometimes, we would try something out of our wheelhouse. We also include "Did you know?" sections throughout the book. These provide interesting trivia we learned along the way that we hope will spur conversations either on the trail or at the pub.

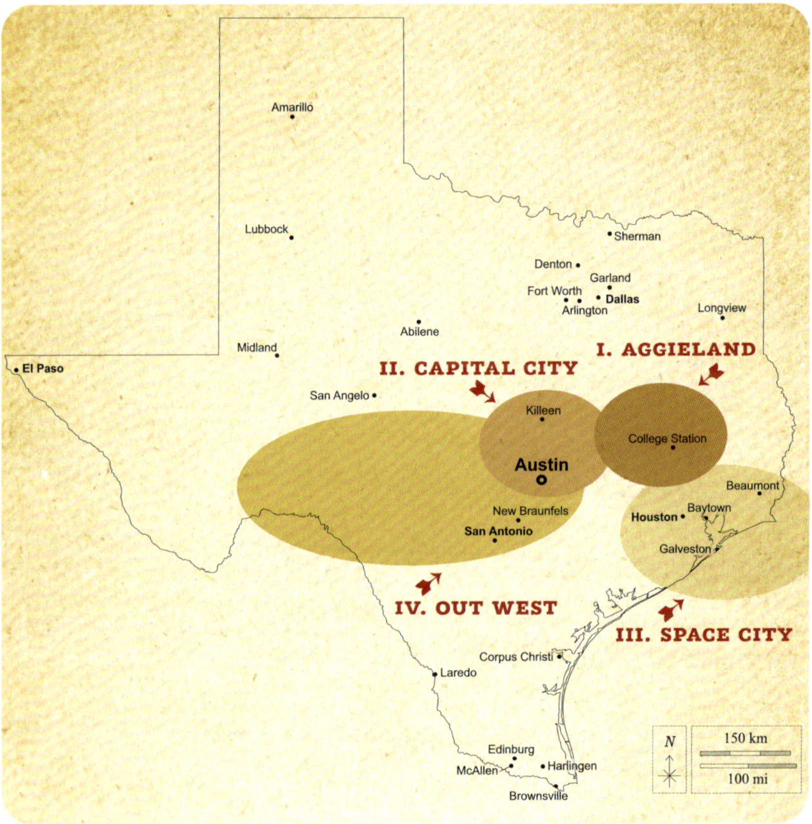

Map of the hikes.

Background map from https://d-maps.com/carte.php?num_car=21639&lang=en

What's our favorite?

Since we started writing this book, the first question everybody asks is, what is your favorite? This was hard to answer because we loved the diversity of every place we visited, but here are our top three hikes and brews:

Hikes

- ★ Big Bend National Park (nothing else like it)
- ★ Lost Maples State Natural Area (great views)
- ★ Inks Lake State Park (hidden gem, lake hike)

Breweries

- ★ B52 Brewing Company (great beer in a wooded setting)
- ★ Lone Pint Brewery (outdoor seating, live music, tried-and-true beer)
- ★ Save the World Brewing Company (a nonprofit, all-Belgian beer!)

Although we visited twenty-five breweries while writing this book, we still didn't get to all our favorites. Here are some of the popular beers we love and didn't have a chance to visit at their source.

- Electric Jellyfish—Pinthouse Pizza Craft Brewpub, Austin
- Dallas Blond—Deep Ellum Brewing Company, Dallas
- Devil's Backbone—Real Ale Brewing Company, Blanco
- Ye Olde Christmas Ale—Saint Arnold Brewing Company, Houston
- Thirsty Goat—Thirsty Planet Brewing, Austin
- Houston Haze—SpindleTap Brewery, Houston
- Juicy IPA—(512) Brewing Company, Austin
- Redbud—Independence Brewing Company, Austin

A Jabberwocky and a Tornado Shark at Lone Pint Brewery.

- Friday IPA—Martin House Brewing Company, Fort Worth
- Rahr's Original—Rahr & Sons Brewing Company, Fort Worth
- Rodeo Clown Double IPA—Karbach Brewing Company, Houston

We hope you enjoy reading this book as much as we enjoyed writing it. Along the way, we were joined by several friends who wanted to experience the perfect day firsthand. Tom and Lou Blinn were constant companions, completing about half the hikes in the book. Friends and family Paul, Bob, Laura, Sarah, Don, Elizabeth, and Wyatt also joined us along the way. Drop us a line at hikes&brews@profpubs.com if we missed any great places. We may run into you one day on the trail or with an ale. Cheers!

SECTION 1

CLOSE TO AGGIELAND

Aggieland, or the Bryan-College Station metro area, is a growing area centered around Texas A&M University. Sitting between Houston, Austin, and Waco, it allows easy access to cities, but there are also some really nice hiking trails and breweries. In this section, we explore seven of each, all located within one hundred miles, making for an easy day trip.

2

LOCALS ONLY

Just the facts

- ★ **HIKE:** Lake Somerville State Park, Birch Creek Unit, Ledbetter
- ★ **BREWERY:** Blackwater Draw Brewing Company, Bryan
- ★ **DATE:** September 14
- ★ **LENGTH:** Just under 6 miles
- ★ **TYPE:** Out-and-back
- ★ **RESTROOMS:** Yes
- ★ **TIME:** 2:55
- ★ **STEPS:** 11,827
- ★ **RAMBLERS:** Jay, Sarah, and Hercules

On a beautiful September morning, Jay, his friend Sarah, and her dog Hercules were ready for some fresh air. We decided to reduce our driving and keep this day-trip local. Located less than an hour from College Station is beautiful Lake Somerville. Neither of us had ever been there, so we decided that this was a must to knock off our list. Our first choice was whether to enter at the north end of the lake, called the Birch Creek Unit, or the south end, called the Nails Creek Unit. The two sides are technically connected if you are up for a 13.4-mile one-way hike. We were not, so we chose the Birch Creek Unit, which is slightly closer to College Station.

Lake Somerville is a state park, so we got to enjoy all the amenities you expect with a state park including flushable toilets, a visitor center, maps, and free entrance with a state park pass. If you are not up for tackling the thirteen-mile Lake Somerville Trailway, there are a variety of short trails that you can chain together to create an itinerary of your choosing. We went left from the visitor center and hit pieces of the Wilderness Run, Cardinal Bend, Bucktail Run, Cedar Loop, Beautyberry, Bluestem Bend, and Eagle Point Trails. We had Sarah's three-legged dachshund, Hercules, with us, so we kept our hiking lengths moderate in case someone ran out of gas.

Did you know?

Dachshunds were bred more than three hundred years ago in Germany to hunt badgers. There are both miniature dachshunds (less than eleven pounds) and regular-sized ones, and they have one of three coat varieties: smooth, long, or wirehaired. They are one of the most popular breeds in the country, ranking twelfth out of 196 in popularity by the American Kennel Club.

We started off walking through a grassy area quite far away from the lake. It was pretty and featured open fields, wildflowers, tall grass, and scrubby trees. Sarah and Jay found it interesting that they had both moved to College Station about five years ago, and this was the first time that either of them had been to Lake Somerville. This was also true for Deb, who has lived in town for more than fifteen years, and for just about everybody else we had talked to. Why was Lake Somerville so off the beaten trail? It was a glorious day in late summer and there was no one around us. We hiked for several hours and may have passed other Bryan–College Station residents but never knew it.

A tree overlooking Lake Somerville.

Wilderness Run Trail, Lake Somerville.

We started at the park headquarters and headed up the Bucktail Run Trail toward Cedar Loop. It was a gorgeous day, with skeleton-like trees in a sea of grass. Wildflowers, butterflies, and birds abounded in the bush as we made our way toward the water. The morning was warm but not hot, making for great hiking.

For a lake hike, we were surprised by the length of trail between us and the water. Walking through untended fields, we were surrounded by a green landscape dotted with yellow flowers. The sun was shining high in the sky, but this mid-September day had yet to become oppressive. Hercules enjoyed his stroll through the high grass, chasing

View of Lake Somerville.

butterflies along the way. As the temperature started to rise, we longed to reach the lake, and then magically around a bend there it was in all its glory, with the sun shimmering off the water like a spell.

We traversed the park with views of the water as we walked on the Beautyberry Trail, which teased us with lake views but refused to actually lead us to the water's edge. We passed a small family fishing

A small family fishing pond.

pond that just increased our longing to reach the shore. Finally, we reached the Bluestem Bend Trail, which led us to the water's edge.

We walked along the sandy beach, watching the sun glisten off the water. Fish skeletons were scattered here and there across the beach. Outside of a lone RV parked a bit from the water, no one was here. We walked along the beach for a good twenty minutes until we noticed Hercules starting to get tuckered out. Since neither of us wanted to carry him back, we turned around and retraced our steps. Besides, it was getting to be about time for a beer.

Blackwater Draw Brewing Company, Bryan.

Since Lake Somerville is so close to Bryan–College Station, a brewery not to miss is the Blackwater Draw Brewing Company (BWD). BWD has been around Aggieland since 2013 and first opened in the Northgate area of town near A&M's campus. It is now located in Historic Downtown Bryan, with lots of space for small and medium events. The taproom atmosphere is very casual, with picnic tables inside and outside and large warehouse doors opening to North Main Street. A food truck is located around the corner, so it is easy to get some tasty local food to go with your beer. While BWD tried to get out of the food business when it moved from Northgate, the COVID restrictions pushed it back into it. Luckily for us, it still featured the Nemo nachos, which were a favorite from the old location. These nachos, starring ahi tuna, are a great variation on a traditional favorite. BWD is a great place to stop after work, on a football weekend, or at the once-a-month First Friday event in Downtown Bryan. And, of course, after a hike! And you can get BWD brews in the local grocery and convenience stores. The brewery is known for its first brew, a coffee porter. On one of our trips to BWD Jay tried the porter, Contract Killer, which met all expectations, while Deb sampled the Hazy Lady IPA.

Did you know?

PORTERS

While Jay is typically an IPA fan, every once in a while, he will try something different. Porters were developed back in the 1700s in England. They tend to have a dark malt and a top-fermenting yeast. They are closely related to stouts, which were originally stronger porters but are considered a different category of beer these days. They are named after English transportation workers, or "porters," who favored the style.

A Contract Killer and a Hazy Lady at Blackwater Draw Brewing Company.

In addition to the beers we tried, BWD almost always has one on tap called Mulligan, a German Kölsch, and another called Border Town, a Mexican-style lager. The taproom also has several rotating styles and seasonal beers that are not available in stores. Jay's favorite is the winter beer, Ole Saint Nipplaus, which tastes like drinking a candy cane! The brewery has a solid variety of beers and has turned into one of those establishments that the locals frequent and that visitors to Aggieland surely need to try.

Hard-to-find entrance at the Nails Creek Unit.

3

LOCALS ONLY REDUX

Just the Facts

- ★ **HIKE:** Lake Somerville State Park, Nails Creek Unit, Ledbetter
- ★ **BREWERY:** Brazos Valley Brewing Company, Brenham
- ★ **DATE:** January 18
- ★ **LENGTH:** 4 miles, but can be tailored to be as long or as short as you want
- ★ **TYPE:** Loop
- ★ **RESTROOMS:** Yes, several, well maintained
- ★ **TIME:** 1:50
- ★ **STEPS:** 9,857
- ★ **RAMBLERS:** Jay, Deb, and Lou

Lake Somerville has two distinct sections, the Birch Creek Unit to the north, and the Nails Creek Unit to the south. The drive to the Nails Creek Unit is a quick one, taking less than an hour from College Station. Since the lake is close to Interstate 290, it is also easily accessible from Houston and Austin and many points in between. Getting there, we fell into the familiar rhythm of driving the byways of Texas through small rural towns like Snook, Frenstat, and Birch.

We met our friend Lou at the main gate, and Jay went in to talk to the park ranger, who gave him a map and informed him that the bridge that connected the trails to Flag Pond was out. She gave clear instructions that included leaving the park and heading down CR 125 until we saw cars parked along the side of the road. We did this, and as we got out of the car, we noticed a big sign that designated this as a hunting area that required wearing an orange blaze. This was not where we were supposed to be. We drove to the end of CR 125 and didn't find the trailhead. Lou then insisted on leading us. She drove until she found a dirt road that said PR 1226. To her and Deb, that meant "Park Road." It didn't; it meant "Private Road." We traveled up the road to two fenced driveways with big "No Trespassing" signs on them. We turned around and were ready to give up when we saw a small park sign and no cars on the side of the road. Finally, we had found the trailhead.

Cucamelon vines.

We started down the trail, excited that we were the only people in this part of the park. We followed the Nails Creek access road for about half a mile until it connected with the loop trail around Flag Pond. Where the trails connected there were restrooms and a primitive campsite. We had clear views of the lake even though the water level was fairly low, especially for the middle of winter. The trail was wide and flat, with even terrain. It is an exemplary hike for beginners and offers a lot of payoffs. We found several interesting examples of diverse flora along the way, including what appeared to be watermelons or pumpkins growing on vines on a tree. It turns out these are cucamelons. They grow wild in Texas and are edible, with a flavor similar to that of cucumbers. Next time, we will grab a snack.

> ***Did you know?***
>
> **LAKES IN TEXAS**
>
> If you have been in Texas a while, you have probably heard that we have only one natural lake, Lake Caddo, in East Texas. While this may or may not be true, depending on whom you talk to, it is clear that Texas has a lot of human-made lakes. These were constructed mostly in the 1950s by the US Army Corps of Engineers to control river flooding. For whatever purpose they were built, they bring in more fish, birds, and other wildlife to our communities and make for great hiking.

The trail provided ample access to the pond and several houses lining the back of the trail with access to the water, and canoes and kayaks were parked nearby. Walking close to the three-hundred-acre pond, we could see nesting birds take flight as we disturbed their respite. One of the most stunning parts of the trail is a grove of majestic oak trees. It turns out that there are over sixty varieties of oak trees in

Our tree hugging-friend Lou, overtaken by the beauty of a tree.

the world, and fifty of them can be found in Texas. As far as we could tell, the ones we saw were live oaks draped in Spanish moss. Lou was so excited that she ran up and hugged a tree. She didn't come close to getting her arms around the diameter. After that we tried hooking up with the Sehike Thicket Trail but missed the turnoff. As we finished the loop, we decided to head over to the lake and walk along the shore.

When we arrived at the lake, the wind was whipping off the water. We wondered aloud whether wind moves faster across water. According to the National Oceanic and Atmospheric Administration (NOAA), it does. The friction that wind encounters on land, such as trees, rocks, buildings, and so forth, slows down the breeze as it moves across the surface. Of course, that is kind of intuitive, but we started noticing that the more we hiked, the more questions we had about the natural world. It is astonishing how little so many of us know about the natural environment that surrounds us. We hiked the short Rocky Point Trail and Overlook Trail, heading over rocks and boulders to get close to the water. There was a lone group of people kayaking that day and only a few people at the park. As the sun glistened off the water, we appreciated another great Texas hike.

Leaving Lou to her own devices, we drove for less than half an hour from Lake Somerville to get to the Brazos Valley Brewing Company on the edge of historic downtown Brenham. The brewery was started by a group of five family members and friends in December 2013 and then moved to its current space on South Jackson Street. At its new location there is plenty of room to play, and the atmosphere is kid and dog friendly. The taproom has a garage door that rolls open to the patio to let in fresh air and lots of sunlight. In the beer garden there are grassy areas and playground equipment, and a stage along with giant games like Connect 4 and Jenga. The brewery has a regular calendar of community events like Thirsty Thursday Tacos and Trivia, and Poses and Pints/Beer and Yoga.

Since we were there on a national holiday, Martin Luther King Jr. Day (a Monday), the usual food trucks were not parked outside, and no live music was playing. But we wanted to give it a try anyway, and frankly, we were a little surprised when we called ahead and discovered it was open for business. Since we were the only ones there, we were able to have a good conversation with Toni, our bartender. She talked about her time at the brewery and let us sample some of the beers on tap. She also gave us a great recommendation on Mexican food nearby—Los Cabos. A great thing about visiting all these

Outdoor area at Brazos Valley Brewing Company, Brenham.

Left: Our helpful server at Brazos Valley Brewing.

Right: Beers in the playful outside area at Brazos Valley Brewing.

breweries is meeting the people who own and work at them. They all have unique stories about how and why they ended up at their brewery.

The brewery offers a great variety of core beers including a blonde ale, German pilsner, brown ale, and coffee ale. In addition to our samples, Jay tried an imperial stout called Slippin' into Darkness with coffee and cocoa nibs. And for his IPA, he chose the Mama Tried Citra IPA. Solid choice, nice and hoppy with Citra hops that add notes of citrus to the beer. Deb had the tangy Orange Cranberry Belgian Wit and then switched to prosecco. Toni told us there was a lot of prosecco left from Sunday brunch the day before, and Deb was tempted by that. What a great way to spend a holiday afternoon, sitting outside, sipping good drinks, and having fun conversation. We were glad Brenham is just a hop, skip, and a jump away, because we have plans to be back. (Oh, and Toni highly recommends the green sauce at Los Cabos.)

4

THE SNAKE IS LONG, SEVEN MILES

Just the facts

- ★ **HIKE:** Little Lake Creek Trail (and then some!), Sam Houston National Forest
- ★ **BREWERY:** Buffalo Bayou Brewing Company, Houston
- ★ **DATE:** August 30
- ★ **LENGTH:** 14+ miles
- ★ **TYPE:** We thought it was a loop trail
- ★ **RESTROOMS:** No
- ★ **TIME:** 5:25
- ★ **STEPS:** 28,345
- ★ **RAMBLERS:** Jay, Deb, and Sarah

We were out again looking for another nearby hike for a warm August day. This time our friend Sarah joined us. She hadn't done much hiking in Texas and was excited to come along. As we left Jay's house at 8:00 a.m., the temperatures were already starting to creep into the eighties. The trailhead was a short forty-five-minute drive from College Station. We were hiking in the Sam Houston National Forest. We had learned from our previous hikes to visit a local gas station to use the restrooms before going into the forest, since facilities were often few and far between. According to AllTrails, Little

Entrance sign to Little Lake Creek.

Lake Creek is a 6.4-mile loop trail. It starts at the same trailhead as point #3 on the Lone Star Hiking Trail. According to the USDA, the Lone Star Trail is 129 miles long, is meant to be primitive (meaning no facilities), and is contained mostly within wilderness areas of the Sam Houston National Forest. In our experience, this is all correct. The trail started off great. There were only a couple of other daring souls willing to brave the wilderness on a late August day in Texas. We strolled past towering trees and beautyberries around every corner. The landscape was rather flat, and after about a mile, the trail opened up into a small pond. Was this Little Lake Creek? No, turns out it was part of Pole Creek. We ended up crossing Little Lake Creek later. The Little Lake portion of the creek begins north of point #2 on the Lone Star Trail.

This is not actually Little Lake Creek, but instead Pole Creek.

We walked and walked, crossed the road a couple of times, checked trail markers, and finally felt like we had turned the loop and were starting to head back. We came to another body of water. Was this the same one or a different one? We weren't sure. We started walking in one direction, but it didn't seem right. Then we started in another direction. That didn't feel right either. The pine trees were all looking the same. Finally, Deb pulled out her phone, hoping for cell phone coverage, and looked for directions to the trailhead. Somehow, we were seven miles away from the car! With the temperatures climbing into the mid-nineties, this was not a good thing. We still felt pretty good, but it was just past 11:00 a.m. and the sun was starting to beat down on us. We walked back to the second trail and had two choices: retrace our steps or follow the Lone Star Trail back to starting point #3. It looked like we were just past starting point #5, so we figured if we couldn't make it back to #3, we could always go out at starting point #4 and get help.

Did you know?

Prehydration can be an important step to keeping hydrated on the trail and being able to carry a bit less water. We recommend drinking a bottle or two of water (twelve to twenty-four ounces) on the drive over to help you stay hydrated while hiking.

Deb had had it with Jay leading and getting the group lost, so she took the lead. Using her phone, she knew the distance back to the car and would call this out every ten to fifteen minutes to keep us motivated. "Four point seven five miles!" This was the first and last time that Deb would take the lead. As she climbed up an embankment, she saw something on the trail in front of her and yelled, "SNAKE!!!!!" When Jay and Sarah climbed the embankment, there was no sign of the snake.

American beautyberries.

Deb swears it was a six-footer with razor-sharp fangs, and of course we all believed her. On all of our hikes, we saw only two snakes, and neither one was a confirmed sighting.

Did you know?

THE SNAKES OF TEXAS

Our state is home to many different types of snakes, but only four are poisonous: rattlesnakes, copperheads, cottonmouths, and coral snakes. If you are not good at identifying snakes, assume it is poisonous. The best thing to do is stay still or back away slowly if you have to. Snakes tend to be found in tall grass and in holes and crevices around logs and rocks. Be aware of snakes and you should be fine.

When we reached point #5 on the Lone Star Trail, three guys were coming up from that point. They were loaded with a lot of gear, and two of them looked more miserable than we hoped we did. Their leader seemed experienced, so we let them go ahead of us a couple of hundred yards. In all honesty, we were happy that they were now on snake patrol and could warn us of any more reptiles in our path. Jay noted that they were carrying a lot of gear, including backpacks and hiking poles. After another half hour or so, we passed two of the guys sitting by the side of the trail looking like they were ready to pass out. We caught up to their leader about ten minutes later and started chatting with him. Turns out he was a very experienced hiker and told us the Lone Star Trail was famous for being a bit difficult to navigate. This made us feel better about getting lost. His goal was to hike the entire length of the trail in January, and his two friends wanted to go with him. He had told them that if they wanted to do this, they would have to hike with him every weekend to get in shape

Anybody see a snake? Deb thought she saw a snake here. No one else did.

for the trip. This explained the backpacks and hiking poles. We don't know whether they ever made the full trip, and by the look in their eyes we're not sure they made it back out on the trail the next week, but we hope they did.

Finally, we hit the last mile. Deb started calling out every tenth of a mile, cheering us on. After what felt like forever, we made it back to

Left: Crossing a dangerous ravine.

Right: When we got lost, all the trees started to look alike. Had we passed these trees already?

the car. Luckily, Jay always kept a cooler of cold water in the trunk. We each drained several bottles of water and then got into the car to enjoy some air conditioning. We were all happy that we made it out without any serious injuries. After a few minutes, the three guys emerged from the woods. They were as glad as we were to finish the hike.

It felt good to sit in the air-conditioned car and cool down for the drive from Little Lake Creek Trail south to Buffalo Bayou Brewing Company, also known as BuffBrew, in the Rice Military neighborhood just outside downtown Houston. When we arrived, we were struck by how massive the brewery was. Standing three stories high with multiple indoor and outdoor seating options—and even a pet-friendly patio—this establishment was impressive. BuffBrew has been in business since 2011, started by two local Houstonians with a love for craft beer. The business has grown and grown and now distributes kegs and cans all over the state, with the most popular beers

Entrance to Buffalo Bayou Brewing Company, Houston.

being Crush City IPA and Dreamsicle. The brewery hosts a bar on the first floor and a full-service restaurant and taproom on the second floor, with rentable venue space on the third—all with excellent views of the Sawyer Yards and downtown Houston.

Since we had worked up quite a sweat on our very long hike and didn't want to share it and the accompanying smells with other

Enjoying an OMS Warrior with a view of downtown Houston.

drinkers and diners, we decided to continue to sweat it out on the sunny second-floor outdoor patio with a great view of the skyline. With a cold beer and a table in the shade, it was really quite comfortable out on the colorful patio. Deb started with a nice light OMS Warrior, which was cool and crisp, and Jay wasn't ready for his usual IPA, so he started with the refreshing Dreamsicle. He could definitely taste the unique orange and vanilla flavors coming through, which hearked back to his childhood ice cream truck days. Sarah decided to keep hydrating with a house-brewed sparkling water. To wash down our drinks and supply us with some much-needed calories, we decided to try a classic Brewhaus pretzel, which came with a grainy mustard and rich beer cheese dip. The combination was faultless.

Sipping on our beers, sampling the pretzel, and still trying to figure out how we got off our trail, we realized how spent we were feeling.

Outdoor patio at Buffalo Bayou.

Brewhaus pretezel with grainy mustard and beer cheese dip on the patio.

Instead of getting more beers and food, we decided to call it a day, planning to come back to BuffBrew and give it a proper tasting when we had more time and energy, and a little less sweat!

Our wish list for the next visit would definitely include the Tikka Masala Fries and the Montrose Pizza, along with a Hazy Crush City IPA and a Great White Buffalo Belgian witbier. Or maybe the Walkin' on Sunshine Lager and Space Cowboy Kölsch with Smoked Birria Nachos . . . or . . . there are too many choices! We'll be back!

Trail to Piney Hill Spur.

5

NEW YEAR, NEW BEGINNINGS

Just the facts

- **HIKE:** Bastrop State Park, Bastrop
- **BREWERY:** Iron Bridge Icehouse at Neighbor's Kitchen and Yard, Bastrop
- **DATE:** January 2
- **LENGTH:** 5 miles
- **TYPE:** Several trails combined to create a loop
- **RESTROOMS:** Yes
- **TIME:** 2:15
- **STEPS:** 12,100
- **RAMBLERS:** Deb, Tom, Lou, Elizabeth, and Wyatt

On January 2 there was a chill in the air, with temperatures starting in the mid-forties, so we bundled up in layers. The bright sunshine, lack of wind, and brisk pace helped us warm up quickly. Joining Deb, Lou, and Tom on this hike were Deb's twenty-year-old daughter, Elizabeth, and her college boyfriend, Wyatt. Jay was on the East Coast with family. Deb and her family used to take an easy hike every holiday break at Bastrop State Park starting when Elizabeth was just five years old, so this was a great way to keep up the tradition. At the time, Elizabeth was attending the University of

Minnesota, and Wyatt is a Minnesotan through and through; they found the "cool" temperatures downright balmy. Their layers came off and got stuffed in Deb's tiny backpack just a few minutes into the hike.

We parked near the park playground and made our way toward the Piney Hill Spur. We were immediately struck by the stark difference between the fresh pine saplings just starting to grow and the scarred and blackened tree trunks left standing. In September 2011,

Tree damaged in the massive September 2011 wildfire.

a devastating forest fire left its mark on the town of Bastrop and its state park. Burning for fifty-five days and ruining over 1,600 homes, it was the most destructive wildfire in Texas. Bastrop State Park is home to the Lost Pines Forest—a section of loblolly pines separated by more than one hundred miles from the Texas Piney Woods. Over a decade later, the rebirth of the Lost Pines Forest showed us how life continues, even after tragic loss. A fitting reminder of new beginnings on our first hike of the year.

The Piney Hill Spur took us to the Lost Pines Loop, normally a challenging 4.3-mile loop. It was partially closed for maintenance, but we were able to use the Old Road Bed and still get a good five-mile hike in. We stopped first at Fehr's Overlook to find a historic Civilian Conservation Corps (CCC) shelter made of Carrizo Sandstone. There were several other CCC landmarks including a water tower and a drinking fountain that was discovered after the 2011 fire. Lou and Deb may or may not have gone off the trail a bit to get a little closer look at the water tower. As on many of our state park hikes, we marveled at the results of the manual labor of these young men looking for work during the Great Depression.

Did you know?

CIVILIAN CONSERVATION CORPS (CCC)

Part of Franklin D. Roosevelt's New Deal, the CCC was a voluntary work program that ran from 1933 to 1942 for young, unemployed, single men. Up to three million men worked in the program during its life-span and created many features in state parks that we still see today.

Left: Historic CCC shelter built in the mid-1930s.

Right: Historic CCC water tower built in the 1930s.

The hike had good climbs, with an elevation change of four hundred feet, and the surface of the trail varied from hardened clay and rocks to sand, to a red carpet of pine needles. Bastrop State Park provided a good workout and a mental health boost. We highly recommend taking a New Year's hike over the holidays to contemplate new beginnings in nature.

Did you know?

PRESCRIBED BURNS

Even though it sounds counterproductive, fire managers may use this method to control fires. Prescribed burns are basically fires that are set on purpose for a number of different objectives. One goal would be to burn up vegetation or brush that could otherwise later ignite a bigger and more uncontrollable, naturally occurring wildfire. In essence, you are fighting fire with fire.

View of the Colorado River from Neighbor's Kitchen and Yard, Bastrop.

After finishing the hike, we made our lunch and beer stop at the nearby Neighbor's Kitchen and Yard in downtown Bastrop. The restaurant sits atop a hill and has multiple levels of wooden patios overlooking the Colorado River and an old iron bridge, built in 1923 and listed in the National Register of Historic Places. While waiting for a table, you can wander in and out of the small artisan shops that surround the restaurant or just admire the funky lawn art from benches outside. And while snacking and sipping at the restaurant, you can often hear live music on a stage down along the banks of the river. The menu comprised a nice mix of made-from-scratch pizzas, sandwiches, and wraps, something to please everyone.

Iron Bridge Icehouse relics.

Deb with her daughter Elizabeth and her friend Wyatt, ready for a beer.

The Iron Bridge Icehouse, next door to the Neighbor's Kitchen and Yard, provided an interesting variety of brews with names just as interesting. The beer brewing was started by a local group of guys whose boys played high school baseball together, and they opened the Iron Bridge Icehouse in December 2019. Deb tried the light and crisp Yard Dog Kölsch and then the Märzen My Stein—an Oktoberfest beer. Tom sampled the amber Prost Zoiglbier and the Geometric Rye-No, a West Coast pale ale. All the beers paired nicely with our lunch. The beer menu features a lot of flavor-infused beers including a Bastrop Blueberry Ale, an Orange Cream Hopsicle, and a Bourbon Pecan Amber Ale. Best of all, though, was time with family and friends, sitting in the sun, watching the river go by, and looking forward to new beginnings.

6

WE'RE FULL, OR NOT

Just the Facts

- ★ **HIKE:** Buescher State Park
- ★ **BREWERY:** 602 Brewing Company, Bastrop
- ★ **DATE:** September 6
- ★ **LENGTH:** 3.8 miles
- ★ **TYPE:** Out-and-back
- ★ **RESTROOMS:** Yes
- ★ **TIME:** 1:34
- ★ **STEPS:** 7,688
- ★ **RAMBLERS:** Jay, Deb, and Sarah

On yet another adventure, we headed out toward the town of Bastrop with its towering pines and Buescher State Park. The sister park to Bastrop State Park, Buescher features a thirty-acre pond and rolling, hilly terrain. Given a forecast well into the nineties, we were desperate for the cooling effect of a water feature. As we drove the hour and a half from College Station to the park, Deb told us how she had tried to go cycling there in June but was turned away because of occupancy restrictions. Jay started to develop a big pit in his stomach. Why hadn't Deb mentioned this before? As we pulled into the entryway, a large man in a ranger outfit greeted us at the entrance.

Jay knew he was going to have to be his most charming to get us into the park.

"Y'all have a day pass?" the ranger asked.

"No, sir. Do we need one?" Jay replied.

"Yup. Ya see, we're all full till Tuesday."

We couldn't believe it. We had driven all this way and couldn't get in. Sarah looked defeated. I was pretty sure she was done with us. She had had nothing but trouble on her hikes with us. Jay made one last-ditch effort.

"Do you have an annual pass that I could buy?" Jay asked.

A smile came over the ranger's face. "Why sure, sir, just pull up there, and I'll take care of it."

Jay pulled up the car and gave him the information necessary for the annual state park pass. The ranger enjoyed that Jay was a Dr. Jay and made several jokes as he was completing our paperwork. He was one of the first Texas state park employees we had met, and he was what we found to be characteristic of rangers across the state: warm, caring, and professional. We met many park employees on our journeys and found every one of them to be awesome. We encourage spending some time talking to them when you travel. They often provide helpful information about trails, weather, and even the surrounding community.

Did you know?

TEXAS STATE PARKS PASS

This pass is one of the best deals around. If you are planning on hiking around Texas, this is a money saver. For seventy dollars a year (in 2025), you get unlimited visits to eighty-nine parks across the state. This includes

Scenic overlook at Buescher State Park.

park entrance for not only the pass holder but everyone in the car. Some parks charge as much as seven dollars per adult, so these passes pay for themselves in no time. You can buy your pass either at the gate of any state park or at https://tpwd.texas.gov/state-parks/park-information/passes/park-passes.

Our Texas state parks are in great condition, with restrooms in abundance. As we approached the trailhead for the Winding Woodland Trail, we found excellent signage and additional signs along the way providing information on the local fauna. The short 1.5-mile trail was nicely shaded by cedars, and it felt cooler than the actual temperature. After finishing the short trail, we crossed the street toward the Pine Gulch Trail. The landscape opened up and we found ourselves with a beautiful vista of rolling ranchland hundreds of feet below. Next to us, an older man sat in a folding chair lazily throwing a tennis ball to his dog. Sarah, the dog person, was immediately drawn to them and started playing fetch with the dog. As we gazed in awe at the beautiful ranchland beneath us, we struck up a conversation with the man. Turns out he was a retired schoolteacher and had decided to roam from state park to state park. We asked him what his favorite state park was, and he told us Tyler State Park. We made a mental note to check it out in the near future.

Pine Gulch was the more scenic of the two trails. Passing through the pines, we had a gentle breeze at our backs as birds and butterflies darted through the flowers. This area had a bit of hilly terrain, and we went up and down several times. Given the location next to farmlands with houses nearby, we guessed that someone named Buescher must have donated the land for this park. We were right. We learned that back in the 1930s, Mr. Emil and Mrs. Elizabeth Buescher deeded over six hundred acres of land to the state of Texas. We were a little bit worried about taking too long a hike, so we chose to use the Barred Owl Cutoff and headed back after another two-thirds of a mile. After we took this trail, we heard the whirring of industrial air conditioners. What the heck could that be? we wondered. As we rounded the bend, a barbed wire fence stood in front of us, with a low-slung research facility behind it. It looked like we had stumbled onto something out of the TV show *Lost*. Deb only half-jokingly expressed concern that the "Others" were following us, and we quickened our pace and turned a corner back into the forest—to be almost run over

An even better scenic overlook with rolling fields below.

Buescher Lake at Buescher State Park.

by a couple of cyclists. Turns out we were just next to an MD Anderson cancer research facility, but it had put our hearts in our throats. The rest of the hike was rather uneventful, so we headed back to our car and drove around a bit to get a full view of the park. We journeyed over to the lake and viewed the shimmering water in the noonday sun. A couple of people were fishing on the banks and there were two or three kayaks on the lake. There is a small rental area, open seasonally, where you can get your own boat or fishing tackle.

We continued driving north through the park toward Bastrop State Park. As we entered a clearing, we happened upon a family of deer out for their midday hike. The mom, dad, and baby looked at us without fear and sauntered along their way. We slowed down to take some photos and to appreciate the natural world around us. After finishing this excellent hike, we were ready for a beer.

One of the many white-tailed deer we encountered along Park Road.

Just a fifteen-minute drive away from Buescher State Park was the 602 Brewing Company, located in downtown Bastrop. We had all driven through Bastrop on numerous occasions on our way to Austin, but none of us had ever taken a turn down Main Street in this quaint little town. When we found the 602 Brewing Company, we noticed the beautiful brick exterior and the cute shops and eating and drinking establishments lining the street nearby (including the Copper Shot Distillery next door). Housed in a building from 1890, the 602 Brewing Company has veteran brewers, a spacious taproom, and a large outdoor patio—part of it covered and part uncovered. We chose a high-top table under the covering with a fan blowing on all the patrons in its vicinity.

Did you know?

INGREDIENTS

There are four ingredients you will find in almost every beer: barley, water, yeast, and hops. Hops are little cone-shaped flowers that give beer its bitterness and other flavors. There are many different types of hops, which give beers their distinct flavors. Many breweries list the International Bitterness Units (IBU) of their beer on the menu. This can tell you how hoppy a beer is going to be. Bud Light has an IBU of 6. Shiner Bock has an IBU of 13, and Karbach Brewing Company Hopadillo is 65. Check the IBU of your favorite beer. This can help you pick out beers that work for your palate.

The menu had a great selection of food and beers. Our server was very attentive and answered questions and let us sample a few beers before we decided. Jay started with a Drunken Monk Belgian-style IPA, Deb had a Blasphemy Hazy IPA, and Sarah tried a seasonal cider. Deb joked that drinking a beer (at a brewery) on Sunday would have been blasphemous in her distant past, but now it just felt like a religious experience—especially after a vigorous hike. Jay enjoyed the hoppiness of his beer along with the distinct flavor of Belgian beer. Once we were settled with our beverages, food was on our mind. The 602 Brewing menu comprised a mix of southern comfort food and Cajun mainstays. It was hard to decide what to choose. Jay ordered Raymond's Crawfish Chowder and a Greek salad. Sarah and Deb decided to stick with seafood too, and both ordered the 602 Shrimp and Grits with smoked Gouda. Jay appreciated the Cajun spin on a traditional New England chowder in his entrée, and the Greek salad offered some fresh greens. Deb and Sarah were wowed by their traditional southern dish. You can never go wrong with grits. Beer round two was

Above: Front of 602 Brewing in downtown Bastrop.

Left: Patio at 602 Brewing.

Enjoying a Blasphemy Hazy IPA while perusing the menu.

made up of Hoppy Clouds for Jay and another Blasphemy Hazy IPA for Deb, which was heavenly with the shrimp and grits. Before we headed back to College Station, we decided to meander down Main Street toward the Colorado River. Downtown Bastrop is a hidden spot with antique shops, art studios, and charming cafés, and we agreed it was worth stopping to explore more thoroughly in the future. For that day, we had had our fill of beautiful hiking and tasty beer sampling.

7

AN AUSPICIOUS START

Just the Facts

- ★ **HIKE:** Double Lake Trail, Coldspring
- ★ **BREWERY:** B52 Brewing Company, Conroe
- ★ **DATE:** August 23
- ★ **LENGTH:** 3.5 miles but can be 7.5
- ★ **TYPE:** Lollipop—out-and-back with a loop
- ★ **RESTROOMS:** Yes, by the lake
- ★ **TIME:** 1:34
- ★ **STEPS:** 7,688
- ★ **RAMBLERS:** Jay and Deb

With mid-August temperatures at 4:00 p.m. in College Station threatening to surpass the triple-digit mark, weekly walks on hot sidewalks along residential streets were beginning to lose their luster. A Sunday hike in the woods on Double Lake Trail would provide welcome shade and something different. We met at 8:00 a.m. armed with water and sunscreen and hit the road. We had a pleasant drive on TX-30, a country road toward Coldspring, passing more cowboy churches, political campaign signs, and deer corn than you could shake a stick at. We almost missed the small dirt parking lot right off the road about an hour and a half from Aggieland. Luck was

We appreciated the extra shade on our late summer hike.

with us that late August morning, and the temperature was a very comfortable seventy-five degrees when we arrived at the trailhead.

The Double Lake Trail is part of the Sam Houston National Forest, one of four national forests in Texas. It covers over 160,000 acres just east of Huntsville and north of Houston. This massive expanse of hardwoods and whispering pines felt a world away from the bustle of Houston and an easy place to get lost in. According to AllTrails, the trail is 7.5 miles long. We decided that this was a bit too long for a late August hike and planned a shorter 3.5-mile route heading in from the trailhead around Double Lake and back out: a lollipop trail, going in on one trail, doing a loop, and leaving on the same trail.

As soon as we entered the forest, we knew we had picked a good route. Mature trees surrounded the trail and provided a canopy of shade. The smell of pine permeated the forest, and needles cushioned our feet as we walked. It was also noticeably cooler as soon as we left the parking lot. The trail was well marked with trail markers, or blazes, along the way.

Did you know?

BLAZES

Getting lost is not fun and can be dangerous. Many trails in Texas and elsewhere are marked with blazes. These markers are often painted rectangles on trees or rectangle metal markers nailed to a tree. Knowing how to read these markers is important. The color tells you which trail you are on. Make sure to note this at the start of the trail, as multiple trails can start at the same trailhead. Then it is pretty simple to follow. A single straight mark means keep going forward. A mark with

(*continued*)

the right side higher than the left means go right, and a mark with the left higher than the right means go left. Two marks indicate a sharp turn.

Trail marker indicating a right turn.

As we approached the lake, we walked across several natural berms. The sides had been eroded over the years by streams. Since it was the middle of summer, it was bone dry. We learned this trail is popular with mountain bikers, but given the time of year, we were mostly alone for the mile out to Double Lake. This twenty-four-acre lake was constructed by the Civilian Conservation Corps in 1937. Sunlight shimmered off the water, and we instantly felt cooler. The trail meanders around the lake, providing water views the entire time. The near side of Double Lake features a swimming area and restrooms, while the far side is marshier and hosts a variety of nesting birds. Jay had remembered seeing alligators in Huntsville State Park on a previous trip and wondered aloud whether there were any in Double

Double Lake overlook.

Lake. When Jay mentioned gators, Deb's adrenaline spiked; she is not so fond of reptiles. This led to an exhilarating but largely unsuccessful search for gators. We did find an elegant white ibis nesting near the far side of the lake, but the rest of the trip was rather critter-free except for some smaller birds and bugs.

We finished the loop around the lake in front of the swimming area where several kids and their families were enjoying the cool water. The park was largely uncrowded that day. AllTrails and several other websites listed the trail as closed because of COVID-19, when in fact it had opened about a month earlier. As we stopped for a water break and scanned the surrounding pines and soothing lake, we realized this was the perfect day for our hiking adventures.

Great place to sit lakeside.

Outdoor seating at B52 Brewing Company, Conroe.

After this successful hike, we headed west toward Conroe, home of the B52 Brewing Company. Lodged on more than seven acres of pine-shaded land, this was an idyllic outdoor setting to find a picnic table and cool off with a beer. With our love of nature, we tried to seek out breweries with outdoor seating spaces, and this one was perfect. We found a high wooden table and stools under an awning with ceiling fans overhead and a nice view of the property. The shade and fans were glorious, and it was fun to watch families and groups of friends playing horseshoes and other lawn games off in the distance.

This newer brewery emphasizes that it is "too good to ignore," and that catchphrase is fitting. The taproom was large and simply situated, and the server was happy to chat about the offerings. The day we were there, they were running a beer and chip combo. The beers on tap ranged from IPAs and stouts to a good selection of sours. Jay started with a Taeda, a New England IPA. Fitting, given his Rhode Island roots. Oh, and he picked a bag of Fritos. Deb chose a sour beer, the Fruit Tart: Raspberry, Pomegranate and Sage, and went fancy with a bag of Gardetto's. For their second round, Jay tried a spicy stout, the Timaeus: Tetrahedron, and Deb stuck with another sour, the Smoothie Tart: Boysenberry, Key Lime and Gardenia. We were pleasantly surprised by the complexity of each of the brews we sampled. As of this writing, the taproom was offering over twenty different beers ranging from pilsners to oatmeal stouts. Beer sizes range from eight- to sixteen-ounce drafts, growler fills, and six-packs to go.

Did you know?

Untappd is social networking for beer drinkers. This great app lets you tag the beers you drink and give them ratings, and allows your friends to see what you're drinking. You can see overall ratings for each beer to help you choose, and the app lets you know what beers places have on tap. Jay used this app to catalog all his beers during our adventures. Find it for free at your favorite app store.

While we loved the brewery and its setting, one of the most striking features of this adventure was the food truck on the premises. The Bright Relish food truck was straight out of Chicago, literally. Deb, who has family in Chicago, knows her way around a Chicago-style

Left: "Meal deal," a Taeda and a Fruit Tart with a bag of Gardetto's at B52.
Right: Chicago-style dog and fries from the Bright Relish food truck.

hot dog, and this was the real deal. She ordered one (celery salt, poppy seed bun, and all) and struck up a conversation with the Chicago Cubs–capped owner, Ed, from Lemont, Illinois. He gave her a hard time when she asked whether he had any vegetarian options for Jay, who at the time was a pescatarian. Ed said, "Not until Vienna Beef starts making one." Jay got fries. Man cannot live on beer alone. B52 has hosted a variety of food trucks. As of this writing, a pizza and BBQ food truck are more or less permanent. We recommend checking the website before you go to find out about current offerings and any other special activities that are scheduled.

What a perfect hiking adventure. Shade, serenity, and sunshine defined this hot Sunday in August.

8

MOTHERS IN ARMS

Just the facts

- ★ **HIKE:** Mother Neff State Park, Moody
- ★ **BREWERY:** Bare Arms Brewing, Waco
- ★ **DATE:** September 19
- ★ **LENGTH:** Approximately 4 miles
- ★ **TYPE:** Loop trail, strung together across separate trails
- ★ **RESTROOMS:** Yes
- ★ **TIME:** 1:31
- ★ **STEPS:** 8,303
- ★ **RAMBLERS:** Jay and Deb

As we were driving to one of our hikes, Deb blurted out, "I wonder who started the state parks? I bet it was a woman." Jay asked her why she thought that, and she said, "Because women have all the best ideas!" Turns out she was right! The first state park in Texas was started by Isabella Neff, better known as Mother Neff. Her youngest son, Pat Neff, became the governor of Texas. When she passed in 1921, she donated six acres of land to the state to become a park. Governor Neff donated the rest of the family's land, totaling 250 acres, for what became the first state park in 1937.

Entrance to Mother Neff State Park.

Heading a bit west of Waco on a fall day, we were excited to get another state park under our belt. We had avoided traveling to Mother Neff before because it had a fairly short trail system, but given an ankle injury of Deb's, it was perfect for a shorter hiking day. Heading over from Aggieland, we passed through the small towns of Chilton, Eddy, and Moody. As we drove through pastureland, it didn't feel like we would find a state park until a copse of trees popped up along with the park entrance gate.

As we drove into the park, it became clear that Mother Neff was a jewel of the state park system. We approached a very well-kept visitor center with a small museum dedicated to Mother Neff, Governor Neff, and the CCC, which helped build this park. Consulting our handy park map, we plotted out a route to hike all the trails in the park. With part of the park closed because of flood damage and another area closed pending development, only about four miles of trail existed. While this was not a lot of hiking, it did make it easy to see the entire park in a day trip. We started off on the Prairie Loop Trail toward the Playground Trail. The trail was flat and easy and covered several prairie areas where wildflowers and butterflies abounded. We were quickly struck with how beautiful the park was. After a quick half-mile jaunt, we made it to a fun natural playground with several activities for the little ones. Mother Neff was one of the most family-friendly parks we had visited. With easy hiking trails, a couple of ponds, bird blinds, clean restrooms, and well-kept campsites, this is an excellent place for families and novice hikers alike.

After convincing Jay to leave the playground, we reached an exhibit on the CCC describing who was stationed here almost ninety years ago and how the CCC helped to construct the park. The CCC was one of the great ideas of America. It gave people jobs, got the country out of the Great Depression, and created lasting infrastructure improvements that we are still enjoying today. From there we entered the forest and the Wash Pond Trail.

The trail was well maintained, with bridges over wet areas and steps when the climb got difficult. We passed by the Wash Pond. Because we were hiking on one of the last days of summer, the water level was low, but it was still pretty, with the sun and clouds reflecting off the water. We passed by the Bluff Trail, saving it for later, because we were excited to get to Tonkawa Cave. Past the Bluff Trail Cutoff, we encountered gentle rolling terrain and found the CCC table, a large stone picnic table set in the woods. From there we joined the Cave Trail and headed off in search of its namesake.

Did you know?

The Tonkawa tribe, which numbered close to two thousand members, lived in the area near present-day Waco for hundreds of years. They aligned with Stephen F. Austin to fight the Comanche. Rumored to be cannibalistic, they were slaughtered by rival tribes during the Tonkawa Massacre in 1862, leaving only about one hundred tribe members. Today, they are an officially recognized tribe in Oklahoma.

Wash Pond Trail at Mother Neff State Park.

Tonkawa Cave—the Tonkawa tribe lived in the area from at least the 1500s.

After a short walk, we reached Tonkawa Cave. Jay was able to easily stand in this large natural formation. Certainly, this cave provided shelter from the elements for many people over the centuries. On the other side was a convenient parking lot for those who want to see the cave but are less mobile. From there we retraced our steps and headed toward the CCC Rock Tower. This stone structure provided an expansive view of the surrounding area. We spent several minutes on top watching birds soar in the updrafts and admiring the surrounding wilderness. Given all the nearby pastureland that was cleared for cattle, it was evident what the state park system was designed for—to protect public land for everyone.

CCC Rock Tower—a stone water tower and observation deck from the mid-1930s.

From the tower, we had completed half the loop and it was time to start heading back. We followed the Tower Trail and took a short detour to visit the Bluff Trail, which we had skipped on the way in. We connected to the Pond Trail and passed the historic bell that was used to inform the CCC workers of mealtimes and impending storms. After another half mile, we reached the beautiful Prairie

Prairie Pond.

Pond. Surrounded by daisies and trees, we were alone there. It was serene and calm, and we felt very nurtured. We walked over to the bird blind and watched the different birds come and play in the water. This was an ideal way to end this short but very enjoyable hike.

We drove just thirty-five minutes from the state park to Bare Arms Brewing—a small brewery just off Interstate 35 in Waco. There were not a lot of folks in the taproom on a Sunday afternoon, so we had a chance to chat with the server, Bridgett. She told us this was the oldest brewery in Waco, established in 2015. She also said that it was first owned by three friends who were engineers—hardworking, roll-up-your-sleeves kind of guys—thus the name, Bare Arms. The flagship beers, including a coffee stout, Kölsch, Vienna lager, and New England–style IPA, are always on tap along with several rotating taproom specials. We had a lot to choose from.

Left: Bare Arms Brewing chalk art in Waco.

Below: Bridgett and the beer selection.

In fact, it was so hard to choose that Deb got a flight of six, yes six, beer samples. Of course, she shared with Jay. Her favorite of the six were the Oktoberfest and Block 5. Jay liked the Hazy Horizon, a New England IPA. The Oktoberfest is a lager with a rich malty flavor—perfect for a fall day. And the Block 5, named after the Falcon 9 rocket

A fun flight of beers including 35 Special, Hazy Horizon, and Oktoberfest.

at SpaceX, has a strong rye taste. We ordered food from the Bare Arms Tailgate food truck outside and sat at a booth in the large open seating area in the taproom. Jay ordered a salad with brisket and Deb got two wood-fired fish tacos. We also got a side of beans in beer sauce and a side of roasted corn relish. Other menu items included burgers, nachos, and beer cheese baked potatoes.

We learned that in addition to providing good food and excellent beer, the brewery offers fun community events like a comedy night and improv classes. It is nice to know that just up the road from Aggieland are these two mainstays. If you need a quick and easy day trip, we recommend this combo. Other fun Waco add-ons include Waco Mammoth National Monument and the Dr Pepper Museum.

SECTION 2

CAPITAL CITY URBAN HIKES

Austin, the capital of Texas, offers some of the best urban hiking in the state. With the Hill Country to the west, there is more varied topography, which creates more interesting hikes and plenty of water features. There are also more than fifty breweries in Austin and the surrounding communities, making our capital a great place for a hike and a brew.

Granger Lake.

9

HIDDEN GEMS

Just the facts

- ★ **HIKE:** Granger Lake, west trailhead, Taylor
- ★ **BREWERY:** Rentsch Brewery, Georgetown
- ★ **DATE:** October 18
- ★ **LENGTH:** 6.4 miles out-and-back
- ★ **TYPE:** Out-and-back
- ★ **RESTROOMS:** Yes, by the main gate
- ★ **TIME:** 2:03
- ★ **STEPS:** 10,252
- ★ **RAMBLERS:** Jay, Deb, Tom, and Lou

For this hike, we decided to go off the beaten path and visit Granger Lake. The lake is overseen by the US Army Corps of Engineers and was developed in the 1970s through a damming project to prevent flooding in the nearby area. The upside of the project is a nice hike with great river views. Located a bit east of Georgetown and an hour and a half from Bryan–College Station, this hike is remote but easily accessible from Austin, Waco, Bryan–College Station, and the surrounding areas. There are two options for hiking: a trailhead in Taylor Park and one off CR 496. We chose the latter, which gave us a 6.5-mile out-and-back hike to a primitive campsite. If you start at

Taylor Park, it is possible to hike over ten miles round trip. There is only one trail at this site, the Comanche Bluffs Trail.

We started hiking at 10:00 a.m. On this beautiful sunny day, the temperatures and humidity were already starting to rise. We passed groves of wildflowers on our way to the trail, along with bridges fording culverts of water. Within ten minutes of starting on the trail, we could already see the lake. Although the lake is beautiful, it is not heavily used for recreation given its remoteness. Though it was a gorgeous warm Sunday, we didn't see any boats or other uses of the lake. Even the trail use was sparse; there were only two other cars parked in the parking lot. Truly a hidden gem.

Did you know?

US ARMY CORPS OF ENGINEERS

George Washington appointed the first engineer to the army way back in 1775, and the US Army Corps of Engineers has been in existence as a permanent branch of the army since 1802. The corps has a long history in civilian projects including building lighthouses and piers and implementing flood mitigation. The Fort Worth District of the corps, which oversees Granger Lake, has fifteen lakes across the region under its jurisdiction.

After some early lake views, the trail moved a bit away from the water into a windswept prairie. As we walked through the grass, we stopped in awe listening to the sounds teeming with life across the grass. Insects chirped excitedly, while butterflies swooped from flower to flower, and birds darted in and out of the grass—sometimes dangerously close to our heads. It was clear that nature ruled this area and human contacts were few and far between.

A view on the Comanche Bluffs Trail.

Rope swing by the San Gabriel River.

After enjoying the soundscape for a few minutes, we continued along the trail, which wound back toward the water. Lake views abounded, with nesting birds darting here and there. There was a thin line here between private residences and public land. Houses sat on the ridge above the lake with footpaths down to the water. We passed several kayaks and rowboats along the shore that most likely belonged to the people in the houses above. Not a bad place to have a house. After about an hour we reached the primitive campsite and the end of the trail. There were a couple of groups that had clearly camped there for a night, and a small group of mountain bikers also passed us at this spot.

San Gabriel River.

By now, we had left the lake behind and were on the San Gabriel River, which flows into Georgetown and the much more famous Blue Hole in Lake Georgetown. We chatted with one of the campers, who told us that they had boated in the night before rather than carrying their packs and supplies down the trail. We found a ladder and a rope swing over the river and dared each other to take it, but no one was up for the challenge. Deb wanted to touch the water, but with the steep embankment she almost went head over teakettle trying to get there. In her younger years she might have tried out the rope swing into the water. As we turned around to head back, we gazed wistfully at the water, vowing to come by boat if we visited again. We retraced our steps back to the cars, ready to explore a new brewery and discuss our travels over a couple of brews.

From our hike, we drove about thirty minutes west toward Georgetown to find another hidden jewel—the Rentsch Brewery. Rentsch, named after father-and-son owners David and Andrew Rentschler, opened in September 2015 in the style of a German beer garden. Appropriately, the first beer they brewed was a Hefeweizen.

The brewery is in an industrial area of town and holds one of the only large outdoor spaces for gathering. The outdoor patio was filled with a variety of tables and bars and seating areas, most shaded by an impressive old tree. The taproom was made up of a small bar and a handful of tables and chairs, with two bikes suspended from the ceiling, but when we were there the taproom was not open to the public. We did show up at the brewery on a special day, though. A small wedding was happening near the beautiful tree just below us. It was so lovely to witness a family celebrating.

Did you know?

GERMAN PURITY LAW

The five-hundred-year-old German Reinheitsgebot, or purity law, is the oldest food safety law still in existence. It requires that beer be made with only four ingredients: malt, hops, yeast, and water. While this has been loosened over the last few years, it is still a point of German pride. Prost!

Lunch of champions: Cheetos paired nicely with a Monkey Rentsch at Rentsch Brewery, Georgetown.

Like other breweries we visited in fall 2020, this brewery had to offer food to keep its establishment open. Cheetos count as food! In addition to snack bags of food, the brewery brings various food trucks on the premises and allows you to bring in your own meals as well. Cheetos and chips weren't going to be enough to pair with our beers, and we weren't in the mood for the barbecue from the food truck, so Lou went and picked us up some tacos from a nearby stand. Tacos and beer are perfect partners. As of summer 2023, a food truck is available there every evening.

Deb's first beer was the Hefeweizen. Served in a plastic cup, it was nice and crisp, something she could drink year-round. Jay tried the IPA and was impressed with its hoppiness. Of course, hoppy makes Jay happy. When we were contemplating our next beers, the father of the groom came over and bought us our next round. We could tell he was so happy about the day and just wanted to share the joy with everyone at the brewery. Deb tried the Weizenbock next and liked the rich flavor, and Jay made a bold move by ordering the Russian imperial stout. Like many of the breweries we visited, Rentsch Brewery offers core beers, specialty beer, and a rarity series. Beers can be ordered in either ten-ounce or sixteen-ounce drafts. Overall, we were pleased with the beers from this relatively new brewery, but most impressed with the idyllic outdoor setting—our own hidden gem, a Texas beer garden.

10

FALLING FOR MY BETTER HALF

Just the facts

- ★ **HIKE:** McKinney Falls State Park, Del Valle
- ★ **BREWERY:** Hold Out Brewing, Austin, and Live Oak Brewing Company, Del Valle
- ★ **DATE:** October 4 / March 14
- ★ **LENGTH:** Just under 5 miles / just over 6 miles
- ★ **TYPE:** Several loop trails
- ★ **RESTROOMS:** Yes
- ★ **TIME:** 1:45 / 2:03
- ★ **STEPS:** 9,232 / 11,235
- ★ **RAMBLERS:** Jay and Deb (Paul for beers) / Jay, Deb, and Don

OCTOBER 4

Starting early on a Sunday morning, we drove two hours from Bryan–College Station to McKinney Falls State Park, a site tucked just past the industrial area of the Austin-Bergstrom International Airport. Driving in, we were amazed to find a wilderness area just beyond the urban sprawl. We pulled up to the park gate and showed our pass. The ranger asked whether we had a reservation, and since we didn't, she told us that a couple who walked their dogs there every weekend weren't coming, and she let us in. Fortune was shining on us. We learned our lesson, though, and vowed to never come to a park again without a reservation. We entered and parked the car next to the restrooms.

Fed by Onion Creek, the park is known for its falls. At the trailhead we started off on a short walk to the Lower Falls. As on many of our state park hikes, we were rewarded by incredible scenery just a few steps from the parking lot. Almost as soon as we started the hike, we found ourselves on a huge slab of limestone that resembled the face of the moon, with craters filled with water. We followed several groups of people walking to the falls, and we were quickly impressed. Even after a long, dry summer the falls were in action, with a deep pool below. We spent a few minutes marveling at the beauty of the falls before deciding to hike over to the Upper Falls. We followed the Picnic Trail to the Rock Shelter Trail, crossing over a section of El Camino Real. This ancient road is famous across Texas and stretches from Mexico to Louisiana.

Did you know?

El Camino Real de Los Tejas is a 2,500-mile trail that runs from Mexico to Louisiana. A former trade and military route, it is marked throughout much of Central Texas.

We passed several of the park's landmarks, including an eight-thousand-year-old rock shelter that had been built by Native American tribes, and Old Baldy, a one-hundred-foot-tall bald cypress—not to be confused with Mount Ol' Baldy at Garner State Park. The history of McKinney Falls is a sordid one. The land was previously owned by Thomas McKinney, an original colonist with Stephen F. Austin. He was a slaveholder and lost most of his fortune after the Civil War.

The "fall" of McKinney Falls.

Swimming hole.

Luckily, he donated his lands to the state so that all people can enjoy this natural wonderland.

The Upper Falls felt like Eden on this warm early fall day. Visitors bathed in the cool spring waters, warding off the rising temperatures. The trees surrounding the falls were lush and green. We all looked at each other and smiled. This special place and terrain were a world apart from the piney woods of the Sam Houston National Forest.

While strolling around the falls was enjoyable, it wasn't really hiking. We had walked only about a mile so far, and we would be getting hungry for lunch soon. We decided to do the 2.8-mile Onion Creek hike and bike trail. This trail starts off along Onion Creek with some pretty good water views and meanders through most of the campsite

Skipping across the rocks.

areas in the park. Once you leave the creek, it is a pleasant, flat walk through the woods, but after the excitement of the falls, it felt a little dull. We did pass the remains of Mr. McKinney's horse trainer's cabin along the way, which was an interesting historical reminder. Given our time constraints, we realized that we hadn't visited more than half of the park. We vowed to come back to see the park in a different season and check out the other trails.

MARCH 14

Five months later we finally made it back to McKinney Falls State Park, this time with Deb's brother Don. It was a cool morning just after a strong storm had passed through, giving the park an ominous look. Starting again at the Lower Falls, we crossed by the pitted limestone, now filled with rainwater, and over to the falls, where a shallow water crossing was necessary to reach the trails.

Wading in the stream.

The ruins of McKinney's gristmill.

The trails on this side of the falls chain up together in a nice loop. We hiked out on the Homestead Trail followed by the Flint Rock Loop Trail and the Williamson Creek Overlook Trail. Together they make for just under a six-mile hike. From the first few steps, it was evident that these trails were much more interesting than the ones on the other side of the park. Ruins of McKinney's holding, including the gristmill and the old homestead, provided an interesting view of the history of this area.

McKinney's old homestead.

Williamson Creek Overlook.

We were just recovering from a deep freeze that had blanketed Texas a few weeks before and were delighted with the signs of spring that were starting to show. While most of the trees were still barren, the grass was a brilliant green, reminiscent of Ireland or the Shire. The Williamson Creek Overlook Trail didn't disappoint, with stunning views of the creek from a hundred feet above.

All told, it took about two hours to complete the three trails on this side of the park. Hardy hikers or those with several hours on their hands could certainly do both sections of the park in a day, but if you have to choose, this is the better route. After two hours of sibling silliness between Deb and Don, we were all ready for a beer and the completion of another successful hike.

Tucked behind Better Half Coffee and Cocktails on Fifth Street is a relatively new brewery near downtown Austin. Hold Out Brewing provides a good amount of parking and lots of shaded outdoor picnic tables for drinking and dining. We had a reservation, and our timing worked out so that Deb's husband, Paul, and their dog Madison could join us for beers and brunch. For some reason, Deb still can't remember the name of the brewery. She regularly refers to the place as Hold 'Em, Hold Up, and Hold It, until she finally gets to Hold Out. Despite the name confusion, it was an easy Sunday drive from McKinney Falls State Park to this brewery in the heart of the city.

Hold Out Brewing sign in Austin.

A Red Bread Redemption at Hold Out.

Jay ordered the Black Is Beautiful and a Koala Takedown, and Paul tried a Carlita. Deb had a Red Bread Redemption. The beer flavors were just as unique as their names. The Black Is Beautiful was a beer with a purpose, raising money for social justice, and the Carlita was a pleasantly hoppy Kölsch. We loved that several of the women employees at Hold Out helped design some of the brews. The brunch menu had a number of great options, but the item that caught our collective

Trying the Koala Takedown.

eye was the roasted beets with creamy feta and avocado, sprinkled with pistachios and a zesty dressing. We couldn't get enough of this unique side. We also thoroughly enjoyed the spinach and artichoke pimento side that came with crispy lavash chips. This was not your typical brewery or brewery fare. Hold Out has a great beer list and features beers in tasters, half pours, and full pours. The menu changes often and features collaborations with other breweries. It also has a nice selection of ciders along with four-packs and six-packs to go.

Another brewery that is just a ten-minute drive from McKinney Falls State Park, and even closer to the Austin-Bergstrom International Airport, is the famous Live Oak Brewing Company. Texas beer drinkers are used to seeing Live Oak cans line the shelves at local grocery stores like H-E-B and Kroger. Surprisingly, it has been brewing beer since 1997. It was hard to believe this was our first time at this brewery, given how long it has been around and how often we have driven so near it. What is striking when you arrive at the brewery is the expansive live oak–shaded, multitiered biergarten with picnic tables and a carpet of leaves strewn about. It was a pleasantly cool day when we were there, but even in the summer the trees likely offer great protection from the sun and heat. An added bonus is the adjacent disk golf course. If we hadn't just had such a good hike, we might have grabbed a Frisbee from the back of the car and started playing.

Live Oak Brewing beer tank in Del Valle.

Old Tree Hugger, Beer Garden Pilz, and Black Is Beautiful under the live oaks.

We ordered our beers outside the taproom. Deb had a Beer Garden Pilz, while Don sampled a version of Black Is Beautiful. Meanwhile, Jay tried an Old Tree Hugger, a barley wine. The nice thing about Live Oak Brewing Company is you know exactly what you are getting: authentic German beer. It also offers Rauchbier or smoked beer. This follows a traditional German style, and if you haven't had it before it is worth exploring. To help wash down the brews we sampled some real-deal German fare from the Black Forest food truck on the premises. Deb and Don tried the Schnitzelwich, a breaded chicken cutlet on a pretzel roll topped with red sauerkraut, and crisp pickles on the side.

Shady outdoor biergarten.

Did you know?

BARLEY WINE

No, you are not drinking wine. Barley wine is beer. It is called that because it has a high alcohol content and complex flavors. To make barley wine, the brewer uses a lot more barley and, to balance the sweetness, more hops. Bigfoot ale from Sierra Nevada Brewing is a nice example of this style that is available in the spring. Try it the next time you are out. You will not be disappointed.

While we enjoyed just stopping in for a quick beer and a bite to eat, we noted that the biergarten would be a great place to hold an event. It was hard to believe we were so close to the city of Austin and all the hustle and bustle of an international airport and still felt so tucked away in a peaceful tree-adorned twenty-two-acre setting. Next time we visit, we will gather a group of friends, grab the Frisbees, and plan to stay a little longer.

11

URBAN WILDERNESS

Just the facts

- ★ **HIKE:** Barton Springs Greenbelt, Austin
- ★ **BREWERY:** Austin Beer Garden Brewing Company, Austin
- ★ **DATE:** October 11 / August 20
- ★ **LENGTH:** About 5 miles
- ★ **TYPE:** Varies depending on the trail
- ★ **RESTROOMS:** No
- ★ **TIME:** 1:51 / 1:00
- ★ **STEPS:** 8,520 / 5,986
- ★ **RAMBLERS:** Jay, Deb, Tom, and Lou

OCTOBER 11

With twelve miles of trails in South Austin, the Barton Springs Greenbelt has some of the best urban hiking you will find in the United States. Run by the Austin Parks and Recreation Department, the greenbelt features a series of entry points throughout the city. Since it is hard to see all of it in one day, we decided to visit twice.

On our first hike, we planned to start out on the Capital of Texas Highway and hike back to Zilker Park. Deb's husband, Paul, was kind

Trail under the MoPac Expressway.

enough to offer to drop us off at the trailhead. With Paul behind the wheel and Deb navigating, we knew that nothing could stop us. We were wrong. A few minutes later, Deb had directed us wrong—which is why she lost her position as direction giver. While she has an eye for photography, she is not our most intuitive navigator. We pulled over at the trailhead where several cars were parked and headed down the trail. Just a few steps in, the hustle and bustle of the highway were gone as we entered an urban paradise. Just steps from the highway was a bloom of green. We hopped across moss-covered rocks with the cars on the overpass sounding like a waterfall above us. We remarked at how many times we had driven on this highway and had no idea about the secret garden below.

Did you know?

AUSTIN PARKS AND RECREATION DEPARTMENT (APRD)

Dating back to 1928, the APRD has preserved land for public use throughout the city. From splash pads to disk golf and the Barton Springs Pool, there is something for everyone. As spectacular as they are, they are even better in partnership with the Austin Parks Foundation. This nonprofit, supported largely by Austin City Limits (one of our favorite events), provides funding for dozens of park and trail improvements throughout the city.

On this early October day, the air was warm, but the oppressive heat had finally receded for the year. We hiked down into the basin ready for some water views but found only a dry riverbed with a lonely rope swing swaying in the breeze. Many people would be dismayed by this lack of water, but not Lou. She jumped from rock to rock, enjoying the adventure of hiking somewhere that was usually covered by water.

Dry riverbed along the Barton Springs Greenbelt.

We followed her and hiked in the riverbed rather than on the trail, becoming more and more dismayed as she told us a story about chiggers. These microscopic mites live near water and leave a horrible bite. We were happy not to encounter any.

We continued along the rocky path for a couple of miles and finally

Beware of chiggers; luckily a lack of water reduces the risk.

joined some wooded paths with a sandy trail. Our goal to reach Barton Springs was looking less likely as the day went on. The upper stretches of river were covered in white crushed stone. We had a reservation at the Austin Beer Garden Brewing Company at 1:00 p.m. Checking our handy map, we texted Paul and arranged for him to

Violet Crown Trail.

meet us at the Homedale trailhead about two-thirds of the way to Barton Springs. We promised to come back and hike more of the trail, and ten months later, we kept that vow.

AUGUST 20

Ten months later, this time in August, Deb and Jay started at the pay lots in Zilker Park. Jay was belting out his favorite Duran Duran song, "Girls on Film," in anticipation of our upcoming visit to Austin City Limits. The path here was easy to find and well marked. It started off with a trail marker at mile 0 of the Violet Crown Trail and headed into a wide sandy path, with dense green foliage on either side. Just about ten minutes from the trailhead, we approached striking rock cliffs facing the right-hand side of the trail.

Given its proximity to Zilker Park, this section of the greenbelt was more well trafficked than the generally empty section near the Capital of Texas Highway. We passed what appeared to be groups of new

Rock formations along the trail.

Barton Springs.

graduate students on an orientation hike. Eventually we reached the water. It was nice to see a rope swing with actual water beneath it, in contrast to our last visit.

Upriver a bit, the water did get shallow quickly. We were once again impressed with the clearness of the streams and took off our shoes and soaked our feet in the water. Deb had sprained her ankle earlier in the summer, so it was good to take a break. And with Barton Springs' cool year-round water temperature, it felt great to be cooling off on a day that was quickly approaching the nineties. Given Deb's still healing ankle, we decided to take it easy and keep the mileage to a minimum. We completed a very pleasant three-mile round trip before returning to the car and heading to the next brewery.

The Austin Beer Garden Brewing Company, also known as ABGB, has a philosophy: Beer Makes It Better. It really does. What is so

A Day Trip pale ale and Industry pilsner at Austin Beer Garden Brewing Company (ABGB), Austin.

Madison, one happy dog at ABGB.

marvelous about this brewery is not only the beer, but the multiple dog-friendly outdoor patios, the indoor setting with live music, and the food. We would go to ABGB even if we weren't ordering beer! The expansive beer garden is not far off South Lamar in South Austin and is usually bustling with locals.

The beer menu has "Always" beers and "Sometimes" beers. On our visit, Deb ordered a Day Trip pale ale from the Always menu and Tom tried the Industry pilsner. Jay had to sample the double IPA, Luxury Liner, from the Sometimes menu. Other Always choices include a helles, an IPA, and a preprohibition-style pilsner. The food menu had so many choices—even a lot of vegetarian options. You can't go wrong with a pizza or the seeded soft pretzel with pimento cheese. But the muffaletta—oh my. And don't get us started on the Reuben. You really can't go to Austin without hiking the greenbelt and lounging on the patios at ABGB. And if you have one, take your dog! ABGB has received national recognition for being voted best in the country at the Great American Beer Festival three years in a row (2016, 2017, 2018).

Did you know?

WHAT THE HELLES?

ABGB has a helles-style beer called Hell Yes. What is this? you might ask. It turns out that helles is a German-style lager beer that is bright pale yellow. It should be a bit sweet with just a hint of bitterness. This delicate and very refreshing beer is a great choice on a warm summer day.

Bull Creek.

12

WATER DOGS

Just the facts

- ★ **HIKE:** Bull Creek Greenbelt to District Park, Austin
- ★ **BREWERY:** Austin Beerworks, Austin
- ★ **DATE:** November 8
- ★ **LENGTH:** About 4 miles
- ★ **TYPE:** Varies depending on entry and exit points
- ★ **RESTROOMS:** No
- ★ **TIME:** 2:00
- ★ **STEPS:** 7,900
- ★ **RAMBLERS:** Jay, Deb, Tom, and Lou

As the weather cooled off in November, it was time to get the group back together and hike in Austin again. This time we chose another Austin parks gem, Bull Creek. On the map this is listed in several ways, including Bull Creek Greenbelt Upper, Lower Bull Creek Greenbelt, Bull Creek Preserve, Bull Creek Park, and Bull Creek District Park. What you need to know is that all the trails connect and make for a great hike. It is located northwest of downtown Austin, and the easy accessibility to the city means the trails can get busy. Where Barton Springs Greenbelt was fairly dry when we were there, Bull Creek was full of water and teeming with birds and other wildlife.

Trail along Bull Creek.

It was a chilly November morning, and the sky was threatening rain, but as soon as we started on the trail it was like entering the Garden of Eden. The trail follows both sides of the creek, and several areas allow for crossings. The water finds a way to move through the creek. From deep crevasses in the limestone to waterfalls and shimmering pools, this was definitely a water hike. The leaves on some of the trees were even changing color, giving us the feel of fall as we walked along.

Did you know?

WATERFALLS

There is just something magical about waterfalls. Any hike with a waterfall or two always has more hikers. But did you know that there are ten different types of waterfalls? They are classified by the way they descend and include fun names like horsetail, cascade, cataract, and punchbowl.

One of our favorite things about Texas streams is their rocky bottom. Unlike mud or sand, it makes for crystal-clear water. No matter how deep the water was, we could see to the bottom of it. After a while, the hike moved a bit away from the stream to a rock-covered overhang. With water dripping down the walls and the rock covered in moss, it was substantially cooler than the surrounding area. Even though we were there in the fall, we knew this would be the perfect refuge during the oppressive summer months too. Large rocks from long-ago landslides dotted the trail and set up fun obstacles in our path.

As we approached Bull Creek District Park, the number of people around the trail increased. Many were posing for holiday cards and other family pictures, and some were just gathered for picnics. At the park we heard a loud splash and turned toward the water, where a

Dripping overhang.

Jay and Tom try to move a boulder out of the way.

dog was swimming with a retrieved tennis ball, returning it to his owner, and waiting for another throw. We stopped and watched them for a few minutes. The man would throw the ball and the dog would go flying into one of the nearby pools, always finding the ball and returning it. We could see the joy in both the dog's eyes and in his owner's. We felt the same way. This is a special area that lifts your spirits and makes you say wow, what a great day!

Just a ten-minute drive from our hike was the Austin brewery staple—Austin Beerworks (ABW). The brewery has been around for over ten years now, and you can't miss that big letter *A* about anywhere you go. These are the cans you see in every Austin grocery and convenience store and in stores around the state. One thing about this establishment that really resonated with us is that it cares not only about the quality of the beer, but also about promoting quality

Outside Austin Beerworks, Austin.

of life for its employees and for the people it serves. This whole hiking adventure was about getting out there to really experience life, so it felt fitting to support this brewery.

When we arrived, we picked one of the red picnic tables on the bright outdoor patio. The outdoor seating had shade coverings and large ceiling fans to keep us comfortable. The cheery colors surrounding us just made us happy to be out on a sunny Sunday. As with a lot of other breweries, food was available from a food truck. The truck at ABW is called CAN-tina, and it offers nice tacos and burgers. We ordered chicken tacos and queso and chips.

The taproom has a long list of beers with the expected core beers, seasonals, and taproom exclusives. However, with only six core beers and thirteen seasonals or exclusives, this is a great place to find

Tasty tacos from a nearby taco truck.

something new. Deb started her beer order with Pearl Snap, a classic German-style pilsner. Pearl Snap can often be found in Deb and her husband's beer fridge in the garage, so it wasn't new to her. But there is something special and different about drinking a beer so close to where it was made. Deb's next beer was the Heisenberg wheat beer,

A+ day on the patio enjoying a Petite Mutants and a Heisenberg wheat beer with chips and salsa.

which had a hint of banana flavor. Jay tried the Petite Mutants, a nice sour stout. The beer orders came with chips and salsa, which were nice to munch on while we waited for our food order. We give this well-established brewery an A+. It was a fun atmosphere and an all-around good experience!

13

RAISING THE DEAD

Just the Facts

- **HIKE:** River Place Nature Trail, Austin
- **BREWERY:** Lazarus Brewing Company, East Austin
- **DATE:** November 22 / August 20
- **LENGTH:** 6.4 miles out-and-back with options
- **TYPE:** Out-and-back
- **ENTRANCE FEE:** $10 per hiker
- **RESTROOMS:** No
- **TIME:** 2:40
- **STEPS:** 12,522
- **RAMBLERS:** Jay and Deb

This was another trail that we did twice. We went the first time in November. We got a late start and had to leave to make our brewery reservation and didn't end up seeing the whole trail. So, nine months later, on a ninety-seven-degree day in August, we decided to go back and do the whole thing. We were glad we did. River Place Nature Trail is about twenty minutes west of downtown Austin in a tiny, hilly neighborhood adjacent to the Colorado River. Three trails make up the nature park: Panther Trail (Lower and Upper), Little Fern Trail, and Canyon Trail. This is where some planning is important. From the Panther trailhead to the Canyon trailhead is 3.2 miles, one way.

An up-and-back will run 6.4 miles, without doing Little Fern Trail, which is probably the prettiest part of the hike. Depending on your time and fitness level, there are several options. You can park a car at both ends and hike only one way. The easiest would be to start at the Canyon trailhead and hike out to the Panther trailhead with a side trip to see the Little Fern Trail. This is mostly downhill and still covers all of the trail. We did not do this. We started at the Panther trailhead and hiked up to the Canyon trailhead and then walked 0.9 mile on the paved road to the Little Fern trailhead and followed that back to Panther. This allowed us to see all the trails but do it in around 5 miles instead of 6.5, which was very welcome on a hot, humid day.

Lower Panther Trail started with a good information sign and a platform to view the small lake, which was full of turtles. They are fun to watch and get you in the mood for spending time in nature. As you start hiking, you notice immediately that it is very well maintained. There are logs to prevent erosion on the sides, chains to help with water crossings, and steps—lots of steps, 2,736 to be exact. You will be cursing at these steps before the end of the hike.

The first part of the trail hugged the creek and provided some nice water views. Several Boy Scout projects had fun names for various features, along with good informational and navigational signs. Just about every quarter mile is marked with a sign indicating the distance to the trailheads.

Did you know?

PANTHERS

Panther Ridge is named after the panthers that used to live in this area. Panther, puma, cougar, and mountain lion are all different names for the same animal. This fact is courtesy of the trail marker by Quinn for his Eagle Scout project.

Rocky start along the Lower Panther Trail.

As you reach the Canyon trailhead, the hike starts to climb. There are long stretches of trail with dozens of steps at a time split up by short flat areas and even some declines. Along the way, the trail comes close to a golf course in several areas. The sound of carts and of clubs whacking balls does take away a bit from the feeling of being deep in nature. Enjoy the views as you climb. Where most hikes have a payoff at the end, this trail just ends at another trailhead on the street without much to see. There were some great views along the way with benches and other relaxing places to stop. This trail was fairly well trafficked, so expect to see other hikers on a regular basis.

Some of the 2,736 stairs on the Lower Panther Trail.

"Noggin' Knocker Tree"; watch your head.

Our favorite Boy Scout–named feature was the "Noggin' Knocker Tree," which obstructed our path on the way up. At six feet five inches, Jay needed to be careful as we approached. There was even a thoughtful first aid kit posted on the tree after the Noggin' Knocker for those who were not as careful. We are not going to lie; this trail was challenging in the summer heat. If you calculate about twelve steps in a flight of stairs, the trail was the equivalent of 228 flights of stairs! Compare this to the Empire State Building, which has 1,827 stairs up to the 102nd floor observation deck. Needless to say, when we got to the end of the Canyon Trail we were gassed and not looking forward to repeating our journey. The woman working at the trailhead took one look at us covered in sweat and recommended taking the shortcut back. We were glad we did. After walking down a sidewalk and passing a few dozen multimillion-dollar homes, we were back on Little Fern Trail.

Sun-dappled water feature.

This short trail hugged a stream and had some small waterfalls and water crossings. Being near water made Deb happy. Compared to the main trail, there was almost no one hiking on it. Even though we were pretty tired and getting dehydrated, it was so peaceful that we were able to enjoy it. In less than a mile we hit Panther Junction and were out of the woods about fifteen minutes later. We are looking forward to doing this one again sometime, but probably after the temperature drops below eighty degrees.

Just over a thirty-minute drive across town from River Place Nature Trail is a relatively new brewery in East Austin. The Lazarus Brewing Company is near a number of interesting bars and restaurants that have come to life in the last few years on this side of town.

Outside Lazarus Brewing Company, Austin.

What started with the All Souls Ale in Montana in 2010 has now become a cool brewery in the heart of the city, serving beer, coffee, and tacos, founded in Austin on Christmas Eve 2016. One owner of the brewery (named Christian) is a former pastor, and religious themes abound—from the building's artwork to the brewery and beer names, and a mission to improve the community. The brewery website quotes Saint Arnold (AD 640): "From man's sweat and God's love, beer came into the world." It's comforting to know that beer has been a part of people's lives for so long.

Drinking a Double Predestination near the barrel room.

Outside the small taproom were different outdoor seating areas with shade, misters, and fans. When you sit outside, you have a nice view of all the wooden beer barrels inside. Sixth Street in Austin has an infamous reputation, but don't let the brewery's location there fool you. On the east side of Interstate 35 the vibe is very chill. Even though the brewery is on a pretty busy road, we were tucked away in the back and nicely sheltered from street noise.

On the blue-sky afternoon we visited the brewery, we were joined by Deb's husband, Paul, and her daughters, Abigail and Elizabeth, who were in town for the start of their Thanksgiving break. We all ordered a nice mix of tacos with *migas*, eggs, avocado, and beans. And of course, chips and guacamole. The beer list is long, with sixteen beers on tap, all with less than twenty parts per million gluten. Deb started with a grapefruity American IPA called Walks on Water and Jay had the bold Double Predestination. The beer names started us all off on conversations about past experiences with church and religious education. Given her background, Deb can tell you everything you need to know (or don't want to know) about predestination. Soon, though, we changed topics and just discussed our favorite podcasts. One we all agreed on was Crimetown.

Dad jokes on hikes and breweries

"Don't procrastinate going to a brewery—hop to it."

"The walk there is twenty minutes, but coming back is an hour. The difference is staggering."

"We've found the walk is faster when you don't have Yuenglings with you."

—Courtesy of the authors' friend Derek Halling

Deb's second beer was called Beartooth, a huckleberry pale ale with a nod to the brewer's Montana days. It had a smooth and simple taste. Jay tried the award-winning Amandus, a Belgian strong ale with a

The bar at Lazarus Brewing Company.

nice banana and pear flavor. We liked the brewery so much we decided to purchase some of the glassware and cans of Prodigal Pils to go. We ended our visit by reflecting on the liveliness of the East Austin community and the part that Lazarus Brewing Company plays in helping to make it a better place. It has also now added a second location in North Austin near Mueller.

SECTION 3

SPACE CITY AND VICINITY

H-Town, the Bayou City, Space City—whatever you call it, America's fourth largest city is famous for many things, from NASA to the Astros and Beyoncé. Until now, it has not been known for great hiking. From beaches to alligators to historical sites, there is some world-class hiking within an easy drive of Houston. And of course, all close to some incredible craft breweries.

Loblolly Trailhead.

14

HOUSTON, WE HAVE A . . .

Just the facts

- ★ **HIKE:** Huntsville State Park, Huntsville
- ★ **BREWERY:** Southern Star Brewing Company, Conroe
- ★ **DATE:** October 25
- ★ **LENGTH:** 7.5 miles—multiple trails around the park
- ★ **TYPE:** Out-and-back
- ★ **RESTROOMS:** Yes, by the main gate
- ★ **TIME:** 2:54
- ★ **STEPS:** 14,988
- ★ **RAMBLERS:** Jay, Deb, Tom, and Lou

While Houston is not known for its hiking, we were excited to discover nature spots around one of America's largest cities. Huntsville State Park is the closest state park to Aggieland, an easy hour's drive away, mostly on the deserted Highway 30 and an easy hop, skip, and a jump from Houston. With a nice cool, overcast morning, we were ready to put some miles behind us. The park features Lake Raven, which is right in the center. It is a popular place to camp with both the RV set and the scouts. After driving in through the main gate, we parked near the Loblolly Trailhead.

Our first decision was which trail to take. Two trails circumnavigate the park: the Triple C Trail (in honor of the Civilian Conservation Corps, of course) and the Chinquapin Trail. Tom and Jay reviewed the map, and we decided on the Chinquapin Trail, which was a bit shorter at 6.9 miles but also gave us some great views of the lake. We headed out on the trail with the trees towering above us and the undergrowth only two to three feet high, giving the forest an open feeling. Huntsville State Park butts up to the Sam Houston National Forest, so the terrain is similar to hikes there. We were happy to be in a state park with good maps, clean restrooms, and rangers along with nicely constructed walkways that kept our feet dry over the wet areas. Both this hike and the Triple C hike are rated as challenging. This appears to be because of the length rather than any technical skill or elevation. If you can walk seven miles, then you can do this hike.

Did you know?

Chinquapin is the name of several species of trees in the beech family. This includes the chestnut tree. While the grand American chestnut trees have almost become extinct, the dwarf chestnut can still be found throughout the southern United States. When Jay discovered this, he broke out with his rendition of "The Christmas Song." Not quite what you want to hear in a forest in October.

After a mile or so of hiking, we reached the lake. A berm had been built to control the water and provide a path across. As we climbed up the berm, we could see stunning views of the lake to our right. A man paddled a small boat, and there was a church service across the water. Other than that, it was a quiet Sunday morning, with birds nesting along the shoreline. We breathed in the serenity of the

Raised path on the Chinquapin Trail.

View of Lake Raven.

moment as Jay told the group that the last time he had been here was with the Cub Scouts. The boys had gone fishing on the pier, and a plucky alligator kept eating every fish they caught. The gator must have thought he was at an all-you-can-eat buffet. Try as we might, however, we did not spot another alligator on this trip.

As we entered the forest again on the other side of the berm, we ran into an athletic older woman whom Jay recognized from his neighborhood. It appears she had the same idea to get out of College Station that we did on this cool fall day. This hike can easily be done on your own, as the trail pops in and out of the forest and provides lake views along the way, with very few isolated stretches. We passed by the historic CCC-constructed dam and spillway along our path. Interestingly, the CCC unit that developed this part of the park was all African American. Their legacy survives today in several projects around the park, including a lodge.

Looking for alligators in Lake Raven.

We finished by taking the short Loblolly Trail for less than a quarter mile back to the car. We thought about visiting the Lone Pint Brewery in Magnolia, but Tom was rightly concerned that all the people who were attending the Renaissance Festival there would be packing the place. So we headed off to Southern Star Brewing Company instead. Someday we would make it to Lone Pint.

The Southern Star Brewing Company in Conroe has been around since 2007, so we were pretty familiar with its brews that we've seen in the grocery store. What we did not expect to see was an unpretentious building settled into a simple landscape tucked not far off Interstate 45. The Sunday afternoon we showed up coincided with a gathering of Volkswagen enthusiasts, with at least ten vintage

Gathering of Volkswagen enthusiasts at Southern Star Brewing, Conroe.

Volkswagens parked in front of the brewery and owners happily sipping and conversing with each other.

To get our beers, we headed upstairs to a top floor taproom that overlooks the grassy lawn. Beer barrels serving as bar tops gave the spacious room just the right amount of charm. The brewery has year-round, seasonal, and limited-release beers, so there was a lot to choose from, and there was also a nice selection of swag. A brewery tour is offered every Saturday at 2:00 p.m. and 4:00 p.m.

Deb started with the Southern Brunch citrus shandy and then tried the seasonal Oktoberfest, for the win. Jay tried Old Major, a Russian imperial stout. This dark beer was brewed for the Houston restaurant Flying Saucer's twentieth anniversary and is aged in Buffalo Trace bourbon barrels for ten months. At 12 percent alcohol by volume (ABV), it is one to be sipped. A lighter second choice for Jay was the Korova Milkshake IPA. It is brewed with lactose, vanilla beans, and lots of hops and tastes somewhat like an orange creamsicle.

Old Major, Southern Brunch, and Korova Milkshake IPA at Southern Star Brewing Company.

Expansive lawn area in front of Southern Star Brewing Company.

We carried our plastic cups down the stairs and outside to a picnic table on the expansive lawn. Food was offered on-site by a young couple making tacos and quesadillas to order under a tent near the lawn. There was some nice music booming in the background. Given that the landscape was so open, cloud cover was perfect on this warm fall day. Overall, this easy-breezy hike and low-key brewery were ideal on a Central Texas fall day. No, Houston, we didn't have any problems.

15

SNOW AND SNAKES

Just the Facts

- ★ **HIKE:** Lone Star Trail, Trailhead #6, Montgomery
- ★ **BREWERY:** Copperhead Brewery, Conroe
- ★ **DATE:** February 20
- ★ **LENGTH:** As long as you want—we did 4.5 miles out-and-back
- ★ **TYPE:** Out-and-back
- ★ **RESTROOMS:** No
- ★ **TIME:** 2:02
- ★ **STEPS:** 9,091
- ★ **RAMBLERS:** Jay, Deb, and Laura

As many Texans will never forget, mid-February 2021 was the time of the great Texas freeze. College Station, like most of the state, was not exempt, as we spent several days with below-freezing temperatures and endured rolling blackouts that it seemed would never end. By Saturday, the weather had passed, and we were getting stir-crazy and ready to get back out on the trail. We decided to head to the Lone Star Trail—with over one hundred miles of trail, there are plenty of places to explore. We decided to start at Trailhead #6, since it was a nice hike from the trailhead to Lake Conroe. We had

Snowy trailhead along the Lone Star Trail.

to make sure Deb got her water feature in. Laura joined us too. As we pulled into the parking lot, we saw something we never expected to see on one of our hikes: snow. The early morning temperature was in the high thirties and expected to get up into the fifties. We knew the snow was soon to be a memory that we would cherish when we were hiking next summer.

Did you know?

SNOW IN HOUSTON

While it is rare, it does happen. Ninety-four times, in fact, since 1881. That is clearly less than once a year, but it does happen. Back on Valentine's Day in 1895, Houston actually got twenty inches of snow! A pretty good excuse to cancel that fancy dinner out.

Chilly start with snow on the ground in the Sam Houston National Forest.

A snow-topped log along the trail.

It was quickly turning into a beautiful sunny day without a cloud in the sky. We headed down the trail with our spirits lifted, glad to be back in the sunshine after the freezing weather we had endured. Winter hiking in the Sam Houston National Forest is dramatically different. After about fifteen minutes of hiking, we realized something that happens in the forest in winter but not in summer. It was wet—really wet. We started off gingerly stepping, trying to stay to the sides of the trail and finding any place that wasn't wet. This technique was met with more failure than success as we scratched our arms and legs on brambles and still ended up with wet feet. After twenty minutes or so of slow progress, we came to a low area with no dry land. We decided to just plow through and after a few tentative steps began to actually enjoy it. It was like being a little kid again and playing in the rain. The

Remote section of Lake Conroe.

water sloshed onto our legs and mud coated everything, but we were having a blast. Our pace picked up, and a few minutes later we had arrived at a remote section of Lake Conroe.

If you are like us and most of your experience with Lake Conroe is driving on Texas State Highway 105 with its party boats and fried fish joints, this is a world away. Waves rippled while the sun glistened across the water, bringing us a sense of much needed calm. We stopped and breathed deeply, stunned at the beauty of the lake. Not a person was in sight as we enjoyed our moment of Zen before heading back to the trail.

From the shore, we continued along the trail, dancing through the rivulets of water that coursed along it with the early spring melt. Along the way we passed burned-out husks of trees that had suffered

The great melting—there was a lot of standing water as the snow melted.

not-so-long-ago lightning strikes. Coming to a large fallen log, Deb decided to try to cross over to the other side. She made it about two steps before falling off the side, luckily landing on her feet. We laughed in delight like children enjoying time in the woods away from their parents. The area near the lake was marshy, giving the feel of a swamp deep in the Louisiana bayou rather than the flats of Central Texas.

We continued along, crossing snowy footbridges and marveling at the height of the trees, some of which stretched two hundred feet in the air. There was such a contrast between summer hikes in Sam Houston and this frozen fun. Sadly, as we continued, the water along the trail kept increasing until we reached a ravine full of water with only a log across it offering safe passage. Remembering Deb's ill-fated attempt to cross a log earlier, we decided to call it a day and head back. We turned around and headed for the car, fully invigorated.

We had to cross several muddy areas while trying to follow the trail.

Outside seating at Copperhead Brewing, Conroe.

A twenty-five-minute drive southeast from the trailhead was the Copperhead Brewery, tucked just off Interstate 45 in Conroe. Established in 2014, the brewery is set up in two buildings (the brewhouse and the pub) with a sheltered patio in between. The brewery offers year-round and specialty brews with scary names like Striker, Bite Me, and Mongoose Slayer. The label artwork is dark themed and stunning.

Out on the patio we found a food truck selling steaming hot pizza, games like Ping-Pong and giant Jenga, and a few picnic tables. The atmosphere outside had a warehouse feel, but inside, the taproom was cozy and warm, and there were a lot of locals, presumably venturing out postsnowstorm like us. Except the giant snake mural on the wall was not cozy and warm, and more than troubling to Deb.

Deb chose her beer quickly in the taproom and settled us at a picnic table outside in the warm sun. She picked the 8.6 percent ABV Athena, a Belgian golden ale. It was nice and smooth and went well with the veggie pizza she ordered from the food truck. Since it was high in alcohol content, she had just one beer and ordered a "to go" pack of four to bring home. Jay started with the citrusy Striker IPA and then tried the

Custom snake artwork inside the brewery.

Black Venom imperial stout. The Black Venom was nice and dark and had all the good chocolate and coffee tastes. These beers were three of the five core beers on tap along with Medusa (a Belgian dark strong) and Bite Me (a blonde lager). The brewery also has several specialty beers on tap that change from time to time. Jay and Laura, who had been steering away from breads and pasta, eyed the pizza longingly. There is something about a beer and pizza combo on a cold day.

Did you know?

PORTER VERSUS STOUT

Cooler weather is a great time for a darker beer. Porters and stouts are two of the most popular dark beer choices, but what is the difference? Porters are made with malted barley, and stouts are made with unmalted roasted barley. Porters tend to be lighter and lower in alcohol content.

Left: Athena and a Striker IPA at Copperhead Brewing.

Right: Veggie pizza from the on-site food truck.

While it was too cold to sight a snake on the trail, it was great to find this snake-themed brewery in such an unexpected place. This day was another example of how getting off the beaten path (and maybe into the mud or a "vipers' den") can offer some great surprises.

16

HERE COME THE TEXANS

Just the Facts

- ★ **HIKE:** Stephen F. Austin State Park
- ★ **BREWERY:** Lone Pint Brewery, Magnolia
- ★ **DATE:** January 9
- ★ **LENGTH:** 3.7 miles
- ★ **TYPE:** Out-and-back
- ★ **RESTROOMS:** Yes
- ★ **TIME:** 1:34
- ★ **STEPS:** 7,688
- ★ **RAMBLERS:** Jay and Deb

"Why have I never heard of the Great Scrape?" Jay asked out of the blue.

"You mean the Runaway Scrape . . . in 1836?" asked Deb. "Only one of the most important historic events to ever occur. Don't you know your Texas history?"

Jay grew up in Rhode Island, and his school curriculum covered a lot of US history but precious little Texas history. When he got to Texas in 2015, he didn't know Sam Houston from Stephen F. Austin. Luckily, the San Felipe de Austin State Historic Site where the Runaway Scrape of 1836 occurred is right next to Stephen F. Austin State Park. Even better, Lone Pint Brewery, which had been on our list to

The Runaway Scrape statue at the San Felipe de Austin State Historic Site.

visit, was on the way home. It was a great way to add a little history into our hike and brewery itinerary.

We headed out on a brilliant sunny January morning to Stephen F. Austin State Park. The Brazos River provides the northern border of the park and the best views around. As water was essential to any early civilization, this was the site that Mr. Austin chose for his first colony in Texas. This is a great hike for families and people new to hiking. Just west of Houston, it is easily accessible to anyone in Harris County and the surrounding communities. With about five miles of trails, every trail is less than a mile long, but they are connected, so it is easy to chain together a bunch of trails to tailor the experience to your group's fitness level and time constraints. We decided to start with the Sycamore Trail and head from there to the Barred Owl Trail.

The trail meandered through hardwoods left mostly bare in the winter. We enjoyed the cooler weather, which is a rarity in Texas. The air was crisp, and the sun provided a bit of warmth when we were not covered by the tree canopy. For the most part, the trails were flat and sparsely occupied. We passed a few groups of campers who had clearly spent the night in the park, but very few day hikers.

Sycamore Trail at Stephen F. Austin State Park.

Did you know?

THE RUNAWAY SCRAPE

The town of San Felipe de Austin was founded in 1823 by Stephen F. Austin as the headquarters for his colony in Mexican Texas. It was occupied for only thirteen years until 1836, when settlers burned it to the ground and fled in fear of Antonio López de Santa Anna, who was making his way up through Texas from San Antonio and the Battle of the Alamo.

After a rainy couple of weeks, the ground was soggy in a lot of places. Luckily, the park included a lot of improved boardwalks and other structures that made hiking easier. A 0.12-mile nature trail provided interpretive signs about the flora and fauna of the park. We passed

Dry feet with a raised pathway along the nature trail.

Brazos River.

a nine-banded armadillo foraging for his breakfast, and dozens of birds singing in the trees. As the river got nearer, the trail started to slope sharply, pulling us toward the water.

The Brazos was brown and muddy from all the rain but still looked majestic. With no development on either side of the river and a nice, steady, peaceful breeze, a calm came over us. Only to be punctured by Deb trying to touch the Brazos. She meandered down to the water's edge, not realizing how slippery it was, and almost went head over heels into the river. After hauling her back up from the banks, we continued across the Ironwood Trail to the Pileated Trail. The park also included a nice wildlife viewing blind adjacent to a park area. We had visited several of these in our travels and were impressed by the birds and other wildlife that flocked there when they didn't know that people were present. Although we could have continued hiking all day, we still needed to learn about the Runaway Scrape, so we finished our hike and headed out to the San Felipe de Austin State Historic Site. The site has a nice museum and several reconstructed

Outdoor area at Lone Pint Brewery, Magnolia.

buildings that make it a worthwhile side trip. It is run by the Texas Historical Commission, not Texas Parks and Wildlife, so your pass will not get you in free, but you may be able to convince them to give you a discount.

An hour's drive from the state park, we were excited to try the Lone Pint Brewery. Jay's favorite Texas beer is its Yellow Rose. The brewery was established by a brother and sister team in 2012, and the place made us feel like part of the family. This beautiful winter Saturday in Magnolia brought out the locals in small groups all over the spacious lawn outside the brewery. Large picnic tables were set up across a grassy square dotted by tall trees. Vendors selling arts and crafts surrounded the perimeter. A live musician was belting out covers on a small stage, and dogs and kids rolled around in the grass. This was one of those temperate January days when everyone wanted to get outside, and Lone Pint was living up to all expectations.

Two food trucks on the premises were setting up to serve food. One was Reveille Barbecue, and we were shocked to see Cousins Maine Lobster. Jay wasn't the only one to have lived in Rhode Island. Deb resided there for seven years before moving to Texas. We talked about

Lobster rolls, yes please! From Cousins Maine Lobster food truck.

how we were both cautious in Texas with ordering our favorite seafood from the East Coast—lobster. But we trusted we would have a great experience trying Cousins Maine Lobster, since it had been featured on so many programs, including the Food Network. We both ordered the succulent Maine Roll and Tots, which paired perfectly with beer.

Deb and Jay both started by ordering a Yellow Rose. It seems anyone who knows about Lone Pint Brewery has tried the Yellow Rose. It was great to finally get one from the source. This SMaSH IPA really is a classic Texas beer, and as many will attest, "I'll remember her forever because I love her so." Deb's second beer was a Tornado Shark, an American strong ale. The name comes from two things many Americans fear, but Deb found it hard not to order another one. Jay's second beer was a Jabberwocky—the monster in a famous Lewis Carroll poem. The only word Jay could say about it was "HOPS!" Lone Pint Brewery was one of those places we would likely go every weekend if we lived a little closer. But it is also a good place to run away to on a sunny winter day. Yellow Rose and Jabberwocky are two of the four core beers along with Zeno's Pale Ale and Gentleman's Relish, an English-style brown ale. Luckily, the College Station H-E-Bs have

Yummy Yellow Rose SMaSH IPA.

started carrying both Yellow Rose and Jabberwocky. The brewery also features several limited-release beers, including the Tornado Shark. The final category is the Zythophile lone hop series. They brew about one a quarter, and it contains just one strain of hops. "Zythophile" means "a person who loves beer." We are both happy to be zythophiles!

Did you know?

"THE YELLOW ROSE OF TEXAS"

"The Yellow Rose of Texas" is a well-known American folk song that dates all the way back to the mid-nineteenth century. It has been sung by Elvis Presley, Willie Nelson, and millions of Texans. The song is referring not to a flower, but to a girl, who was fabled to have helped Texas gain its independence from Mexico. The earliest version of the song is said to be housed in a library at the University of Texas. The lyrics have been changed, and the latest version of "The Yellow Rose of Texas" is also known as "The Eyes of Texas" and is the school spirit song at the University of Texas.

17

SEE YOU LATER, ALLIGATOR

Just the facts

★ **HIKE:** Brazos Bend State Park, Needville

★ **BREWERY:** Braman Winery and Brewery, Richmond

★ **DATE:** November 15

★ **LENGTH:** 9+ miles

★ **TYPE:** Loop, strung together across separate trails

★ **RESTROOMS:** Yes

★ **TIME:** 3:26

★ **STEPS:** 18,239

★ **RAMBLERS:** Jay, Deb, Tom, and Lou

We were in the mood to see some wildlife and decided to head to Brazos Bend State Park. Located south of Houston in Fort Bend County, Brazos Bend is famous for its alligators. Even though Deb is not a fan of reptiles, we assured her that there was nothing to be afraid of and that we probably wouldn't even see any gators. That worked until we saw the entrance sign, when she started expressing some concern.

We made our way in and parked by 40 Acre Lake. The water was a deep blue under the late fall sky, and the day was crisp with a breeze blowing across the water. With no gators in sight, we started hiking on the 40 Acre Trail to the observation tower. Lily pads dotted the

Above: Brazos Bend welcome sign.

Left: Do not feed or annoy the alligators warning sign.

Observation tower with a great view of the park.

lake and provided a comfortable, serene environment. We reached the tower and climbed to the observation deck. The 360-degree view was stunning, illuminating the bayous that ran through the park and the oceans of grass that surrounded us. Unlike at Sea Rim State Park, where the ocean is ever present, at Brazos Bend the water is more subtle, hidden beneath the life it sustains. Yes, water is no less important to the character of this park.

Spotted a gator.

We climbed down the tower and continued on to the Spillway Trail toward Elm Lake. The path was glorious; with water on both sides and the trees draped with Spanish moss, it felt like we were a world away from hiking in the Sam Houston National Forest, and certainly Austin hikes. This felt like the Deep South. Deb was getting more comfortable in the park and suspected she would not see any gators. She was wrong. After a short half-mile walk through Spanish moss–covered trees, we reached Elm Lake. Within a few minutes we spotted dozens of alligators swimming in the lake and dozing on its shoreline. Luckily, most of them were pretty small and didn't seem to care that we were there.

From Elm Lake, we continued hiking to the Nature Center. The park rangers were awesome, as always, and answered our questions about the gators and the history of the park. Turns out there are about 250 alligators in the park. The Nature Center had an excellent educational exhibit with live baby alligators you could pet. The stop here makes for a good break on the long trail between Elm Lake and the Brazos River. There are several trail options from the Nature Center to the Brazos. We took Big Creek Bridge Trail to the Bluestem Trail to Franky's Dam Trail. The reward on these trails was several great views of the Brazos, which we had crossed about ninety miles upstream heading into Grimes County. By the time we got to the river, it was already past noon and Tom was getting hangry. He was less than delighted when Jay told him we were more than four miles from the car.

Did you know?

ALLIGATORS

Many people confuse crocodiles and alligators. Gators have wider, U-shaped snouts, while crocs have more V-shaped snouts. Crocs are also a lot meaner. The easiest way to tell them apart if you're hiking in Texas is to bet on alligators. The nearest crocodiles live in Florida. While most gators in Texas are found on the east coast between Corpus Christi and Nacogdoches, there have been sightings west of Austin and San Antonio.

We headed back on the White Oak Trail to the Hale Lake Loop. Along the way, we passed the Houston Museum of Natural Science Observatory. It was closed because of COVID, but when it is open, it hosts star parties and has a nice museum. We took the Live Oak Trail back, which parallels the southern border of the park and was a straight line back to the car. This trail was also surrounded by water, though we didn't see another gator.

We arrived back at the car and considered visiting the George Ranch Historical Park just up the road. But with Tom starting to forage in the bushes for lunch, we decided it was time to head for the brewery.

Brazos River.

Left: Running Walker pint glass with a Texas Reserve IPA.
Right: Braman tasting and taproom, Richmond.

Just forty minutes' drive from Brazos Bend State Park is the Braman Winery and Brewery in Richmond, Texas. This is the first combination winery and brewery in Texas. The multitalented founder is Joe Braman, whose family heritage in Texas dates back to 1835. The brewery features Running Walker Beer, advertised as "fiercely independent" and displaying a signature logo of a lone hound dog. Joe Braman has made a name for himself not only with the winery and brewery, but also as a dog trainer. As you approach, the venue looks like a large warehouse, but the massive space provides cozy, dim rooms inside with tables and sofas and an expansive outdoor patio with a stage and barrel tables. The winery is on one side of the warehouse, and the brewery is on the other.

We settled outside around a barrel table, since it was such a beautiful day. A bonus was "Easy Sundays" live music featuring Frank Matta. There was such a festive vibe at this place, with a mix of couples, friends, families with kids, and plenty of canine friends too. Some guests brought their own food and others ordered from the

Left: A barrel of fun with Jay and Tom.

Right: El Canton Firewood Pizzeria pizza and two Texas Reserve IPAs.

pizza vendor set up outside—El Canton Firewood Pizzeria from Katy, Texas. We split a Luna Verde—a thin-crust, wood-fired pizza with spinach, goat cheese, mozzarella, and pesto. It was sensational. We were so hungry we got another!

And let's not forget the beer. The brewery offered a nice selection of year-round beers along with some specials and wine barrel–aged sours. Deb sampled a refreshing can of Kölsch and a fruity Berliner Weisse that was on tap. Jay tried the solid Texas Reserve IPA and the spicy stout. We definitely will be back to try the wine. Update, bad news! We did go back in summer 2023 and were told they were closing the brewery. The space is still open from Thursday to Sunday for flight nights and live music, but it is being turned into an event space. Luckily, Houston has no shortage of breweries, so it shouldn't be hard to find a substitute.

Alligators, hiking, friends, pizza, beers, sunshine, and live music. We can't think of a better way to spend a fall Sunday. OK, Deb could live without the alligators.

18

A DAY AT THE BEACH

Just the facts

- **HIKE:** Sea Rim State Park, Sabine Pass
- **BREWERY:** Buckstin Brewing Company, Nederland
- **DATE:** October 30
- **LENGTH:** 5 miles, but can be tailored to be as long or as short as you want
- **TYPE:** Out-and-back
- **RESTROOMS:** Yes, by the main gate
- **TIME:** 1:52
- **STEPS:** 9,755
- **RAMBLER:** Jay

At the end of October, Deb was out of town, and I (Jay) was going to spend the weekend with friends in Anahuac. I decided to do a hike and brew solo. Growing up in Rhode Island and Hawaii, I was itching to be back by the ocean. Looking at the map of state parks, one place stood out, Sea Rim State Park. Nestled between McFaddin National Wildlife Refuge and Sabine Pass, this park of over four thousand acres promised miles of uncrowded beach walking. That sounded like a perfect way to clear my head and kick off Halloween weekend.

I needed to be back in Anahuac for sunset cocktails at 6:00 p.m. so I decided to do the day backward, stopping at the brewery first and then heading out to the shore. Sea Rim is farther away than most of the other hikes, taking about three hours or more to get there, depending on Houston traffic. Luckily, for folks living in Baytown and East Houston it is only about an hour and a half. As I left the peacefulness of Highway 6 for 290, I could feel my blood pressure going up. After living on a tropical island for fifteen years, I am still not used to big city traffic, and driving in Houston is not my cup of tea. It didn't get any better when I left 290 for I-10. The heavy industry of Houston all the way through Baytown was soul crushing. After a brief respite around Anahuac, I was again approaching the refineries of Port Arthur. I couldn't believe I was going to find a brewery out here, but then I turned onto Boston Avenue in Nederland, and everything changed.

All the street parking was free, which is a joy in this day and age. I parked across the street from the Buckstin Brewing Company and walked in. I could immediately tell it was a friendly place. Four guys in their twenties were sitting at the bar chatting with the two bartenders. Some great classic rock was playing on the radio. Next to me was a refrigerator full of sixteen-ounce four-packs of beer to go. The plaque on the table announced that I was sitting in Buck and Elsie's booth,

Inside Buckstin Brewing Company, Nederland.

in memory of James "Buck" Buchanan, who I assume was the founder and namesake of the brewery. The menu was mostly pizzas with a few appetizers, like a hot pretzel. I asked the server what he would recommend, and he told me their pizzas were out of this world. Having faith in him, I ordered a veggie pie along with a Pug Nasty Double IPA since I'm a sucker for clever names. They have a great beer list here, with eighteen house brews and five guest taps offering mostly hard cider. The styles of beer are also vast, including cream ale, Belgian dubbel, helles, Hefeweizen, and even a peanut butter imperial stout.

My server was right, the pizza was fantastic, and the Pug Nasty was a solid IPA. Since it came in at a hefty 9.2 percent ABV, I decided to tone it down a bit on my second round so I could make it to the hike. My server recommended a Bucktober Fest. Since October was almost over, I decided to go with it before this seasonal style was gone for the year. It was nice and smooth and went down easy. When I had finished my beer and almost half the pizza, it was time to hit the road and burn some of those calories off.

Did you know?

ABV stands for alcohol by volume. Technically it is the number of milliliters of pure ethanol in one hundred milliliters at sixty-eight degrees Fahrenheit. Back when I turned twenty-one, there was no ABV listed on beers. That's because it was illegal. From after prohibition up until 1995, breweries could not list the ABV in their beer. When this changed, ice beers were soon introduced, like Miller Lite Ice with the slogan "More of what you want, less of what you don't." I guess that is truth in advertising. Today, it is important to keep an eye on the ABV. It is not uncommon to see a Belgian tripel, a double IPA, or an imperial stout top 10 percent ABV. These are twice as strong as 5 percent beer, so keep track and don't overdo it.

Pizza and a Pug Nasty Double IPA—a winning combo.

As I drove from Buckstin Brewing Company over to Sea Rim, I passed right through the Port Arthur Refinery, and I mean right through. The plant sits on both sides of the road and the pipes go right above where you are driving. "Man, this place is huge," I thought to myself. Turns out that was an understatement. The Port A Refinery is actually the largest oil refinery in North America. It has been in operation since 1903 and has over 1,200 employees, many of whom are more likely to die from a variety of cancers. While it was pretty cool and otherworldly driving through here, it was not the nature experience I had in mind.

Finally, I put the refinery in my rearview mirror, crossed through Sabine Pass, and headed for the beach. I rolled down my window as I drove and could smell the salt air. As I turned into Sea Rim State Park around 2:00 p.m. I knew I was in for a treat. The place was pretty much deserted. After my free entry with my state park pass, I parked

Walkway to the sea.

next to the boardwalk and headed toward the beach. Behind me were three or four RVs with a couple of people sitting in lawn chairs, and in front of me there were a couple of small groups of people. I turned left and for the next 2.5 miles didn't see anyone.

As I left the area immediately in front of the boardwalk, I was surrounded by birds, from plovers playing in the surf, to great blue herons soaring majestically, to gulls laughing at me. I felt the weight of the city immediately lift from my shoulders as the ocean breeze covered my face. Shells in all shapes and sizes covered the beach where I walked, and I picked up a few here and there.

Did you know?

HURRICANES

Sea Rim State Park is at high risk from hurricanes. Back in 1989, Hurricane Jerry destroyed State Highway 87, blocking access to High Island. Hurricane Rita struck in 2005, causing extensive damage. Hurricane Ike also hit in 2008, causing more damage. The park was totally closed until April 2010, a year and a half later, and didn't fully reopen until June 2014.

Left: A calm inlet at Sea Rim State Park.

Right: Birds playing in the surf.

After a half hour or so, an inlet of water crossed my path. Removing my shoes, I found a shallow area to pass. On the other side of the inlet, things were even wilder. It was clear that very few people had come this way recently. Footprints were replaced by deer tracks. It was remote and wonderful. I could see Sabine Pass in the distance,

Shell collection that Jay brought home from Sea Rim State Park.

but no matter how far I walked it never seemed to get much closer. Although the scenery didn't change much, the sound of the crashing surf and the feel of the water and sand on my feet brought a great sense of peace. The beach was very clean, with only the random fishing net or smooth glass washed up from the surf. I could have kept walking forever, but sunset cocktails called, so I turned around after about an hour and started my walk back. When I got back to the car, I had a big smile on my face, two shoes full of shells, and salt caking my legs. I was already thinking about the next time I could get back to the shore.

SECTION 4

HILL COUNTRY AND OUT WEST

Everything is bigger in Texas. We all know this, but it takes driving large swaths of it to have it fully sink in. In this section, we ventured west past Austin and way out to Big Bend to explore some of the more interesting trails in the state. Several of these were weekend trips or longer, but it was definitely worth it!

A view of Inks Lake State Park.

19

SANCTUARIES

Just the Facts

- ★ **HIKE:** Inks Lake State Park, Burnet
- ★ **BREWERY:** Save the World Brewing Company, Marble Falls
- ★ **DATE:** January 23
- ★ **LENGTH:** 4–8 miles, but can be tailored to be as long or as short as you want
- ★ **TYPE:** Loop and out-and-back; easy to tie several trails together
- ★ **RESTROOMS:** Yes, several, well maintained
- ★ **TIME:** 3:33
- ★ **STEPS:** 16,473
- ★ **RAMBLERS:** Jay and Deb

We decided to head out to the Hill Country for this hike. We jumped online about a week in advance and tried to grab reservations for Pedernales Falls State Park or Enchanted Rock, but both were fully booked for the weekend. Consulting our handy Texas state park map, we noticed that Inks Lake State Park was not too far away. Deb remembered some of her friends telling her that this was a good hike. We were able to snag the last reservation slot and were glad we did, since it turned out to be one of our favorite hikes!

Located in the Hill County about two and a half hours west of College Station, and not too far from Georgetown and Round Rock, sits Inks Lake State Park. You know you are there before you get there as you turn off Highway 29 onto Park Road 4. The road climbs into the hills above the Colorado River with a couple of scenic stop-offs along the way. After about four miles of twists and turns, you enter the main gate of the state park. Once you enter the gate, there is a parking lot next to several hiking trails. We decided to skip those trails for now and wound our way through the park to the trailhead for Devil's Waterhole Nature Trail. With Deb's love of the water, we decided to do some light hiking with water views first, followed by hiking on the longer trails at the park entrance later. These can be done in any order, but we do recommend doing both since they are vastly different hikes.

The Devil's Waterhole is one of those trails where you take a few steps and get a great payoff. As soon as we were 0.2 miles from the trailhead, both of our jaws dropped open. Wow! The water was clear and glassy, and the surrounding cliffs made it a quiet place of solace from the world outside. We knew that in the summer this place must be crawling with people, but for now it was just us, a few campers rising from their slumber, and a lone kayaker on the lake.

Quickly finishing the Devil's Waterhole, we connected to the Valley Spring Creek Trail, which climbed somewhat steeply and provided overlooking views of the lake. We meandered around this trail, with each view of the lake more stunning than the one before it. The water was some of the clearest we have seen, and it was easy to pick out the rocks on the bottom of the lake even when it was more than ten feet deep.

As the Valley Spring Creek Trail ended and turned into the Devil's Backbone Nature Trail, we found ourselves on the other side of the lake looking back at the pink granite hills that we had just climbed. Although there was some good topography and ups and downs, this

Solitude by the water on the Devil's Waterhole Trail.

was a pretty easy hike and would be suitable for beginners. We ran into several small groups of people, most of whom appeared to have been camping and decided to venture out for a day hike. A group of women about our age were hiking and asked us to take a photo of them. Lisa from their group was kind enough to return the favor and took this stunning shot.

Did you know?

CAVES

The Hill Country is full of natural caves. If you've driven to from Austin to San Antonio, you have probably noticed the signs for Natural Bridge Caverns. You can also find Inner Space Cavern, Bracken Cave, and Cave without a Name in the Hill Country. If you are hiking at Inks Lake State Park, Longhorn Cavern is close by. This is a state park with nice grounds and some cool CCC buildings. The caverns have been used for a variety of different activities throughout the years, including as a nightclub. Tours of the caverns are available for a fee.

Authors Jay and Deb taking a break.

A bird blind at the end of the Devil's Backbone Nature Trail.

The trail continued around the lake with more awe-inspiring views. We passed two turkey vultures lazily sunning themselves and looking for lunch. They barely recognized our presence as we walked by. At the end of the trail, we got another treat, a bird blind built by Master Naturalists! If you have a dog, it cannot go in. And if you do go in, you have to remain quiet, but it is worth it. We quietly entered the enclosure and were the only people there. It felt like a sanctuary, with dozens of birds flying, perching on trees, and hopping on the ground, oblivious to our presence. We spent about fifteen minutes watching them and then returned to our hike. These three trails together were less than two miles long, but it was an out-and-back, so we ended up hiking about four. If that is all you have in the tank, we would recommend these trails over the other trails in the park given the stunning water views. We were feeling great, so we drove over to the trailhead parking lot.

Rock formations along the Lake Trail.

At the parking lot by the main gate, you have your choice of trails. We took the Lake Trail to the Woodland Trail, to the Connecting Trail, to the Pecan Flats Trail. This created about a 2.5-mile loop. As in all Texas state parks, the hiking maps are excellent. Make sure to grab one when you enter the park and keep it with you while hiking. We were surprised by the change in terrain. The Lake Trail quickly rose above Inks Lake and gave us incredible views of not only the lake but the surrounding countryside. After that peak, the trail moved away from the lake and quickly became much drier.

Ghostly trees damaged by lightning along the Woodland Trail.

As the Lake Trail became the Woodland Trail and the Connecting Trail, the terrain changed to savanna. It wound its way through juniper trees and yucca, with an occasional blast of color from a yaupon bush. A sun-bleached skeleton of a fox was visible from the trail, probably a feast for the turkey vultures we had seen earlier. Several trees burned by lightning gave the trail a ghostlike feel. As the sunny morning turned to clouds, we felt the first drops of rain splash onto our heads, and we were glad we had completed the loop and were back at our car. This was a sensational hike, and the most scenic and varied since we had started. We would like to have hiked all day, but the weather wasn't cooperating, and it was time to check out a new brewery.

A drive of just a little over twenty minutes from Inks Lake State Park to an industrial area of Marble Falls, Texas, takes you to the Save the World Brewing Company, where all profits go to charity. In fact,

Save the World Brewing Company, Marble Falls.

it is a 100 percent philanthropic brewery. On the day we were there the workers told us that all tips were going to a local food bank. Examples of other charities the brewery donates to are Habitat for Humanity, Meals on Wheels, and Food for the Hungry. The brewery was started in 2012 by a husband-and-wife duo, both former physicians who wanted to change their lives and live out their passion—while helping to save the world. The brewery has a True Beerliever loyalty club that gets you a T-shirt and lots of other perks, including your own Save the World glass stored in the tasting room.

The brewery has a selection of celebration and everyday beers, all with meaningful names. Deb's first choice was Agnus Dei (Lamb of God)—a smooth and easy witbier from the everyday menu. Her second beer, also from the everyday, was the Humilus Filius (Humble Son) Belgian pale ale, which was really fantastic. She liked it so much she bought a six-pack to take with her. Jay went with celebration ales. He had a double milk chocolate stout, Gladius (sword) Dubbel, and Sol Vinum, a Belgian golden strong ale on red wine grapes. The staff was very friendly and happy to answer any questions about the beer or the brewery. They told us they distribute beer in Austin, San Antonio, and Waco.

Sol Vinum and Humilus Filius in the outdoor seating area.

The bustling Save the World taproom.

Did you know?

BELGIAN BEERS

For those in the know, Belgium makes some of the world's best beers. Unrestrained by the German purity laws, they have been experimenting with beer styles for centuries. The most famous are the Trappist ales, which are brewed inside the walls of a monastery. This abbey-style ale comes in dubbel, tripel, and even a quad version, with the alcohol content getting higher as you go up. For those looking for something a little lighter, there are the Flanders red, witbier, and Belgian blonde ale. No matter your choice, you can't go wrong with a Belgian beer.

Save the World serves snacks like cheeses and local sausages, but there is also a food truck on-site. When we were there, the food truck was Oh My Pizza Pie with the signature sign on the truck, "Give Pizza Chance." We ordered one ten-inch, wood-fired thin-crust veggie pizza with olives and tomatoes, and a second one with arugula, goat cheese, and balsamic glaze. They came out hot and delicious, served on big white paper plates.

We found the atmosphere at this brewery to be so tranquil. We sat under ceiling fans at a picnic table out on the large, covered patio overlooking a grassy "football field" area where there were even more tables and kids playing at a playground on-site. Some people around us, with their dogs at their feet, looked like they were settled in to hang out for a while. Others showed up with their glasses from previous visits just for a beer before heading on to other Saturday plans. At this brewery, we were happy to be in a different kind of sanctuary, to drink its beer, and to save the world!

Vista Brewing, Driftwood.

20

COUNTRY ROADS

Just the facts

- **HIKE:** Pedernales Falls State Park, Johnson City
- **BREWERY:** Vista Brewing, Driftwood
- **DATE:** March 20
- **LENGTH:** 9+ miles
- **TYPE:** Loop trail, strung together across separate trails
- **RESTROOMS:** Yes
- **TIME:** 3:29
- **STEPS:** 17,097
- **RAMBLERS:** Jay, Deb, Tom, and Bob

Ask Texans their favorite month, and most will say March. The temperatures are usually mild, and the wild bluebonnet flowers are usually starting to blossom along highways and country roads. We were fortunate on this Saturday in March to experience all of that. Tom, Jay, and Jay's friend Bob visiting from New England met up with Deb in Austin, and we all headed west to start our adventure at Vista Brewing. Just thirty minutes from Austin, this brewery advertises fresh air and fresh beer. We agree on both counts.

Nestled into the countryside in Driftwood, Texas, Vista was established in April 2018. It has it all: lush grounds, great beer, and top-notch food. The expansive twenty-one-acre space houses the brewery, a farm, a restaurant, a beer garden, and room for private events. We took a stroll around the grounds and saw chairs set up for a wedding later that day. All the beer is made with limestone-filtered water from the property. The brewery also has satellite taprooms in Bee Cave and San Antonio.

There were a bunch of picnic tables outside on a bed of wood chips near tree swings and Adirondack chairs. Nearby, young families were celebrating a birthday, and the kids were having the time of their life taking turns on the swings. The beer menu is varied and complex. It offers five year-round drafts, a couple of collaborations, and a barrel program where the beers are aged in wine and spirit barrels. It also offers several bottles of a variety of wine barrel–aged concoctions for consumption on the premises or at home. We settled down with our beers, enjoying the sounds of laughter all around us. Deb picked a Kölsch called Adair, an old Texas family name. It was light and fruity and had a nice bubbly quality. Tom tried Revive, an amber ale that had a nice red color and rich taste. Jay ordered the Vista classic, a Destination IPA, and Bob ordered the Fireside, a whiskey barrel–aged imperial stout. On the day we went, the food was from a limited menu and prepackaged, but still quite impressive. Deb had a superfresh kale and butternut squash salad along with a roasted turkey sandwich, and Jay ate the filling butternut squash salad as well. Current food offerings are advertised as farm fresh and hyperlocal and include a cheese board, salads, tacos, and a burger. We knew we had a pretty full day of hiking yet to go, so we each stuck with one beer. But Deb bought a Bee Cave honey wheat four-pack to go. Since Bob had arrived from the much colder temperatures in Massachusetts, he was really warming to our hikes and brews weekend escapade.

Unfortunately, we had made the error of doing brews and hikes instead of hikes and brews, but this was for a legitimate reason. Even though we had booked a month in advance, all the morning reservations at Pedernales Falls State Park were taken. The park gates are

Left: Destination IPA and Adair Kölsch with a view.

Right: Jay and his friend Bob enjoying a Destination IPA and a Fireside imperial stout.

closed from 12:00 to 2:00 p.m., so don't bother getting there early. We took a slow, forty-minute drive from Vista across backcountry roads and still ended up arriving at 1:45. We sat in line waiting for the gate to open and enjoyed watching all the impatient people who got out of their cars to go and try to speed things up. The gate was not opening until 2:00 p.m. Once it opened, we headed toward the falls. While this is not an extensive hiking area, it is what everybody comes to this state park for. In a word, the Pedernales Falls are stunning.

After parking just outside the overlook, we walked down the dirt trail to another overlook just above the Cypress Pool. The vista was breathtaking. On the day we were there the water was flowing over just a couple of sections of rocks, and we were able to walk across to the other side while keeping our feet dry. Tom showed us a video of a day a couple of years before when the river was really flowing, and wow, it can rise dramatically.

Pedernales Falls.

We hiked down to the rocks and carefully made our way across the falls. Numerous pools of water looked inviting for a swim. We had to hold Deb back from jumping in. This part of the falls is off-limits for swimming and can be quite dangerous. For those who are here to take a dip, there is an area farther down the river that is calmer and open. Where we were was great for climbing and bouldering. Since so many of our hikes occurred in the flatlands of Central Texas, we jumped and climbed like little kids on the rocks for an hour or so. We were able to find some springs where the water was literally coming out of the rocks.

Did you know?

PEDERNALES

Deb tried to figure out what "Pedernales" meant, so she Googled it. Google wasn't much help; it said "a river in Central Texas." Actually, it is the plural form of *pedernal*, which means "flint," like the rocks we found in the river.

After a while, Jay grew tired of our tomfoolery and reminded us that we were writing a book on hiking, not playing in the falls. A bit disappointed, we took a last look at the falls and headed over to the 5.5-mile Cypress Mill Loop Trail. After taking a wooded path downhill, we again approached the Pedernales River. This time we were at Trammell's Crossing. Named after T. J. Trammell, a farmer who lived in the area during the 1870s, this was a shallow water crossing. We took off our shoes and slowly made our way across the river. It was slippery, rocky, and up to a foot deep in some areas. Sitting on the other side of the river, gingerly putting our shoes back on our wet feet, we observed a group of twenty-something guys dressed in everything from tactical gear to jeans walk right up to the river and cross with no hesitation. We decided to follow their lead and keep our shoes on when we came back.

Across the river, the trail headed up and then flattened off into a meadow. Butterflies and birds darted from flower to flower, and it was a peaceful place to ramble. Since the twenty-somethings went a different way, we were all alone on the trail, which was a nice contrast to the crowds by the falls. As we walked along, Bob's head filled with

Jay, Tom, and Bob rock climbing at Pedernales Falls.

A natural spring provides fresh water to the surrounding area.

Trammell's Crossing along the 5.5-mile Cypress Mill Loop Trail.

visions of grandeur. He had now been on both a hike and one of our brewery visits, so he decided the book should be "Hikes and Brews with Jay and Bob." Deb was not pleased with this, so he tried changing the title to "Hikes and Brews Featuring Bob." We told him we would think about it, and he started counting his royalties. (He's not getting any royalties.) The path started to climb again and culminated at the

A view from the top of the Cypress Mill Loop Trail.

5.5-Mile Loop Overlook. Clearly, the creative person had the day off when this trail was named. The overlook was breathtaking, though. We gasped when we first saw it. We could see for miles in every direction, without any sign of buildings, cars, or other human development. With beautiful blue skies, this was one of the most amazing places we had been. As we headed back down the mountain, we were just in awe of how gorgeous this park was. This was one of the prettiest and most fun hikes we had been on, and we all vowed to get out on those country roads and come back again soon.

21

THE OSTRICH AND THE MONKEY

Just the facts

- **HIKE:** Lost Maples State Natural Area, Vanderpool
- **BREWERY:** Pint and Plow Brewing Company, Kerrville
- **DATE:** January 29
- **LENGTH:** 4–8 miles, but can be tailored to be as long or as short as you want
- **TYPE:** Loop and out-and-back; easy to tie several trails together
- **RESTROOMS:** Yes, several, well maintained
- **TIME:** 2:56
- **STEPS:** 15,322
- **RAMBLERS:** Jay, Deb, Lou, and Tom

We switched up our typical hiking day when we embarked on a weekend-long trip to the Hill Country. This would be our trial run for back-to-back day hikes. We planned ahead to get our park reservations and a large rental house in Leakey (complete with rocking chairs on a wraparound patio and a massive hot tub), about halfway between the two parks where we wanted to hike.

Front of Pint and Plow Brewing Company, Kerrville.

Because we could get only a late afternoon reservation at Lost Maples State Natural Area, we decided to visit a brewery first. We chose Pint and Plow Brewing Company in Kerrville because of its central location between Austin and Vanderpool, and because we were curious about the name of the brewery. Tucked off a busy road cutting through Kerrville, the brewery thinks of itself as a community center for the town, offering house-crafted beer, comfort food, and organic coffee and espresso. The logo for the brewery was quite a curiosity, with a farmer plowing a field with an ostrich. Inside the taproom, the ostrich imagery was very apparent. Connected to the brewery was a charming coffee shop, and large overhead doors opened out of the taproom to the sheltered patio. We found out that the name comes from brewing beer with water sourced from the nearby Guadalupe River, and the deep agricultural roots in Kerrville. The ostrich theme found its way to the brewery in a number of serendipitous ways, including a 1900s newspaper found in the walls of the brewery advertising ostrich feathers.

Left: Pint and Plow's unique sign.

Below: Ostrich wall art inside Pint and Plow Brewing Company.

We settled on a cozy outside picnic table and ordered our food and beers inside. The brewery had a small but well-crafted beer selection ranging from a lager to a porter, and it also offered beer, cocktails, and wine. It had beer in all sizes, including half pints, pints, pitchers, and a flight of all six beers. The food menu presented a nice balance

"Kerrville is the New Kerrville" sign in the outdoor patio, with a Tchoupitoulas American IPA and The Divide Belgian-style saison.

of meat and nonmeat options, with salads, sandwiches, pizzas, and small plates.

Deb tried The Divide, a Belgian-style saison, which had a nice haze to it. The name is a nod to "The Divide," a nearby rural community on the Edwards Plateau, a strip of land that divides rainfall runoff. Her second brew was the hoppy Tchoupitoulas IPA, named after a local street. The beers paired nicely with the Unadulterated Chicken Salad Sandwich with kettle chips. Jay also sampled the Tchoupitoulas IPA along with the Super Fresh Sandwich and a simple salad. While sipping and sunning out on the patio, we noticed lots of locals coming and going—couples out for an afternoon lunch and business meetings over beer. We really did feel a sense of community at this establishment and felt fortunate to have occasion to make a stop in Kerrville ("the New Kerrville").

Big lunch of an Unadulterated Chicken Salad Sandwich, kettle chips, and The Divide beer.

After we finished our beers and lunch at Pint and Plow, we headed west toward the Hill Country. We were amazed at the number of hotels and motels in Kerrville and wondered what was out here to create such a high demand for lodging. The only answer we got from Pint and Plow employees was a several-days-long folk festival. While this did seem popular, it couldn't have been the only reason people were staying in town. We found out another reason almost as soon as we left and our path crossed the Guadalupe River. The ride from Kerrville to Lost Maples State Natural Area is only an hour, and it cuts through some beautiful country. Riverside parks stocked with kayaks and small waterfalls abounded. After leaving the river, the road runs through pristine ranchland with almost no cars in sight before heading up into the Lost Maples State Natural Area.

We were visiting Lost Maples at a nonpeak time. Much as Inks Lake State Park is built for summer fun, Lost Maples is the must-see place in the fall when the leaves change color. We didn't know what to expect as we arrived in the dead of winter, thinking the leaves would have fallen from the maples some time ago. Maybe this would be a bust. The natural area is situated inside a huge canyon that protects it on both sides. According to information at the ranger station, the canyon protects the flora and fauna from extreme temperatures and appears to be what saved the Uvalde bigtooth maples from the last ice age. As we entered the park, it was like discovering paradise. The sun was shining brightly and the chill that was in the air at the brewery was gone. This is a state natural area instead of a state park, meaning that it is more protected. In this case, it meant that there were only 250 parking spaces in the park, and any camping and restrooms outside the entry area were primitive. On a Friday in January, this was not a problem, as most of the parking spots were empty, with maybe only thirty to forty cars. We drove and parked at the Maple Trail trailhead and started our journey.

Did you know?

TEXAS RIVERS

Water features often make hikes more scenic and interesting. Texas is blessed with several long rivers that start in the northwest part of the state and flow to the Gulf of Mexico. We were lucky enough to hike close to several of these rivers, including the Rio Grande and the Guadalupe, Brazos, Colorado, Frio, Trinity, Sabinal, and Sabine Rivers. The longest river is of course the Rio Grande, coming in at over 1,800 miles, with 1,250 of those miles in Texas. The shortest river is the Comal, at just 2.5 miles and entirely in New Braunfels. You can usually trace a line to a river and its tributaries and ponds and find a great hike just about anywhere.

Bigtooth maple leaves.

We started up the short Maple Trail and found the grove of bigtooth maples. As expected, most of the leaves had fallen to the ground and the ones that remained were brown. We were disappointed but not surprised to see this. The grove of maples is actually small and confined to one area. Luckily, the rest of the park was phenomenal and worth the trip.

The Maple Trail connects to the East Trail, which hugs the Sabinal River. The river offered million-dollar views of crystal-clear water, boulders, and canyon walls along with a roadrunner that joined us on our journey for a while.

It was a perfect day for hiking. Our maps pointed out two upcoming points of interest—Monkey Rock and the Grotto. Jay noted that wherever rock formations were named, he often couldn't really see

A river runs through it—Sabinal River at Lost Maples State Natural Area.

Monkey Rock.

what the formation was supposed to be. This was not the case with Monkey Rock. We headed down the short path to this feature and stopped in our tracks. There in the limestone was clearly a laughing monkey. If it wasn't for the maples, we think this park would be known for the monkey.

We crossed a small stream and walked through several interesting rock formations along the way, including the Grotto, which had water dripping down the side. The air was noticeably cooler here, which is probably great most of the year, but less appreciated on this late January day. A few minutes later, we reached another warning sign and things got serious.

This part of the trail was almost directly uphill. After about ten minutes of heading up, we were seriously regretting doing the brews before the hike. A group of college-aged students were right behind

Left: Deb cliff walking near the Grotto.

Right: Warning sign about the difficulty of the hike—we shouldn't have done the brewery first.

us, so to keep our pride intact, we put our heads down and made it to the top of the hill. On the trail, two points were marked "scenic overlook." The first was just a third of a mile down an out-and-back trail. Sadly, this view was underwhelming. We headed back the way we had come, a bit disappointed, and headed to the second scenic overlook. This one did not disappoint. Panoramic views of the valley with the river below were stunning. They were even nice enough to put in a bench where we could sit for a moment and enjoy it. A bit down the trail was a primitive campsite that was placed perfectly to give unforgettable views of the sunrise and sunset.

From there we headed down the mountain toward the East-West Trail. This was the express elevator back down. As steep as we thought the way up was, this was worse. We were happy we were all wearing our hiking shoes, as the trail was covered with small rocks. We were

The payoff was a great view at the top of the East Trail.

also glad we were not camping and carrying tents and sleeping bags up and down this incline. At the bottom, we reached the East-West Trail, which again brought us next to the Sabinal. Here there were larger shady trees and deeper ponds with several people fishing. You could imagine that these would be fabulous swimming holes in the

Great view of the Sabinal River in Lost Maples.

summer months. We wanted to do the West Trail, but that was just as long and strenuous as this one. Besides, it left us something to come back for in the future. Deciding to leave something in the tank for tomorrow's hike, we headed back to our cars and drove to our rental house in Leakey. We were excited to be able to hike again the next day.

22

HOT AND FRIO

Just the facts

- ★ **HIKE:** Garner State Park, Concan
- ★ **BREWERY:** Blue Star Brewing Company, San Antonio
- ★ **DATE:** January 30
- ★ **LENGTH:** 2–10 miles, but can be tailored to be as long or as short as you want
- ★ **TYPE:** Several short trails across the park from river view to steeper climbs
- ★ **RESTROOMS:** Yes, several, well maintained
- ★ **TIME:** 3:02
- ★ **STEPS:** 16,572
- ★ **RAMBLERS:** Jay, Deb, Lou, Tom, and Laura

We were surrounded by fog when we embarked on our drive to Garner State Park, and we worried that the day might be pretty dreary. We arrived there just before noon as the sun broke through and the clouds moved out. It had turned into a glorious day.

The first thing you notice about Garner State Park is the Frio River. It cuts through the park, providing dramatic views and plenty of summer fun. In fact, it is one of the best tubing rivers in the state. In late January, we saw only a few brave souls who were willing to walk into the river up to their knees. We parked by the Pecan Grove Camping Area and walked next to the river under the skeletal winter trees.

Did you know?

FRIO RIVER OR RIO FRIO

The Spanish word *frio* means "cold," and like many rivers in Texas, the Frio River is spring fed and cool to cold year-round. Running two hundred miles, it flows from Real County until it reaches the Nueces River.

We hooked up with the Blinn River Trail, which was only half a mile long, but in our opinion, it had the most stunning views in the park. Hugging the Frio, the trail brings you close to waterfalls and wading areas. Large rocks were frequently in our way along the trail as we skirted our way forward—sometimes on the trail and sometimes in the river. The crystal-clean, cool water was hard to keep out of, and we had fun playing in it. We were loving Garner already, until we made a mistake.

We were anxious to get some miles under our belts, so we chose the 2.9-mile Frio Canyon Trail. The maps urged us to "experience the vastness of the Frio Canyon," and we were excited for incredible canyon views. Instead, we experienced an hour and a half of walking through prairie. The wide-open trail offered no shade, which wasn't a problem in the winter but could be deadly in the summer. This would be a nice trail to bring kids on who are learning how to mountain bike. However, we would recommend skipping this one and spending your time by the river or in the mountains.

After a relaxing picnic lunch down by the river, we were ready for some altitude. We decided to hit the Crystal Cave Trail, a hike of two-thirds of a mile up the mountain. The ascent wasn't bad, and we made

The Frio River.

The Frio Canyon Trail is not the most interesting trail.

Crystal Cave along the short but steep Crystal Cave Trail.

it up in just about twenty minutes. It was definitely worth it; the cave was thirty feet deep and covered in crystals. The map recommends bringing a flashlight, but like most other people these days, we all had our phones with built-in flashlights. It was much cooler in the cave, and it was like visiting a pirates' hideout. Even at six feet five inches, it was easy for Jay to get in and explore the area.

From the cave, there were a variety of options based on time and fitness level. We followed the Bell Trail to the Rim Trail and got some fantastic views of the canyon. *This* was the place to get canyon views—not the Canyon Trail. There were also some nice views of Mount Ol' Baldy. At the ridge, we decided to split up—Laura and Jay took the Bridges Trail back down to the river so they could get back to the house and get some hot-tubbing in. Lou was fascinated with Mount Ol' Baldy and convinced the rest of the crew to go with her. What happened at this point was not clear. Laura and Jay finished the hike and took a car back to the house. Two hours later, Tom, Lou, and Deb pulled up looking disheveled and confused. Jay asked them how the hike up Mount Ol' Baldy went. It seems they got lost and never made

The great views on the Rim Trail are worth the climb.

it. One trail they took led them to a dead end on the wrong side of a ridge. Cell phones again saved the day, and they were able to find their way back. Besides that small mishap (and a few extra miles), the day had been a winner.

On our way back from our phenomenal hiking weekend in the Texas Hill Country, we drove through San Antonio to try out the Blue

Star Brewing Company. One of the older breweries we visited, Blue Star has been serving an eclectic variety of beer since 1996. It is conveniently located along a bike and walking path called Mission Reach. We saw a lot of foot and bike traffic in this busy little off-the-Riverwalk section of San Antonio. In fact, the brewery founder, Joey, also owns the Blue Star Bike Shop next door, which provides bike rentals for biking around town. Any community that promotes biking and walking scores a star with Deb and Jay.

The creative brewery had great outdoor space with a raised patio wrapped around two sides of the building, some sections with covering. And there was another outdoor patio at a higher level. There is live big band jazz out on the patios every Tuesday night. The great thing about Texas is that you can drink, dine, and listen to music outside most of the year, and the winter months are often the most pleasant.

Did you know?

OLDEST BREWERY IN TEXAS

Our trip through Texas history made us think about the history of beer brewing in the state. According to the Texas State Historical Association, the oldest brewery in Texas was the Western Brewery owned by William A. Menger, which was in operation from 1855 to 1878 nearby in downtown San Antonio right next to the Alamo. If that name sounds familiar, it's because he also owned the Menger Hotel. The brewery was located right behind the hotel and the cellar had three-foot-thick walls that helped keep the beer cool as it was aging. With the German population in Texas, there was a bigger demand for lager beer, which requires cooler and longer fermentation than ales. The oldest still-operating craft brewery in Texas is the Saint Arnold Brewing Company, established in 1994 in Houston.

Blue Star Brewing Company, San Antonio.

We lucked out and were seated right away on one of the lower patios, where we could people watch and enjoy the Texas winter sunshine. Even though it was a busy Sunday at the brewery, the staff was attentive and helpful. Our server answered a lot of questions about the beer and brewery. The brewery offers nine draft beers as well as a barnstormer series of interesting concoctions including several sour beers. Deb ordered the new-to-the-menu Brother X, a Belgian pale ale, and thought it was fabulous! Jay started with King William Ale, a strong barley wine–style ale. Next, Deb sampled a Spire Stout that wasn't her thing, so she went with her "go-to"—a wheat beer. Wheathead was light and refreshing and paired nicely with the fish tacos and salad she ordered. Since Deb raved about Brother X so much, Jay tried that next, and he agreed it was good. He ordered a veggie wrap and we shared a pretzel with beer cheese dip.

Brother X Belgian pale ale and King William Ale on the patio.

This was one of those breweries where we wanted to take some home, so Deb ordered a can of Brother X to go. And not just any can, a thirty-two-ounce can! We know that when we go back to San Antonio, this will be one of the places we'll always want to visit. And we want to try out the Mission Reach bike and walking path too.

Our hiking weekend was a complete success. The Hill Country offered some of the best hiking so far, and the breweries continued to impress us. If you want more than just a day hike, we highly recommend making a weekend of it.

23

WHERE THE STARS AT NIGHT . . .

Just the facts

- **HIKE:** Davis Mountains State Park, Fort Davis
- **BREWERY:** Fredericksburg Brewing Company, Fredericksburg
- **DATE:** April 14
- **LENGTH:** 2–10 miles, but can be tailored to be as long or as short as you want
- **TYPE:** Loop and out-and-back; easy to tie several trails together
- **RESTROOMS:** Yes, several, well maintained
- **TIME:** 1:33
- **STEPS:** 8,652
- **RAMBLERS:** Jay, Deb, Lou, and Tom

Is there anything more exciting to a rambler than the phrase "road trip"? While the majority of Texans live in the central and eastern parts of the state, some of the best hiking is out west. We started our journey by driving to the McDonald Observatory. The University of Texas operates several large telescopes in this region. We met up with our colleague Bill Wren, who heads up the Dark Sky Initiative for the observatory. In short, his job is to convince local government and businesses to use smart lighting techniques to keep the ground lit and the sky dark. He sure is doing his job. The stars in the six counties surrounding the observatory are brilliant in the night sky and helped bring us closer to nature than we had felt before.

From there it was off to Fort Davis. A series of forts from San Antonio to El Paso, each a day's ride apart on horseback, strung along the I-10 corridor. We stopped at Fort Lancaster on the way out, an isolated and beautiful stop run by the Texas Historical Commission. Fort Davis is the best-preserved fort and is run by the National Park Service. It is certainly worth your time if you plan on hiking in Davis Mountains State Park.

Did you know?

NATIONAL PARK PASS

The National Park Service runs more than two thousand recreation sites in the country, with fourteen in Texas. An annual pass is a great way to see these. For just eighty dollars, everyone in your car gets admitted to the park. Going to just Big Bend and Fort Davis would cost fifty dollars for two people, making this a great deal. There are free annual passes for active military, Gold Star families, permanently disabled citizens, and all fourth graders. If you are sixty-two or older, you can get a lifetime pass for just eighty dollars. Check out the National Park Service website for details or ask a ranger.

Finally, we got to the hiking part of our journey. Davis Mountains State Park is probably most famous for its historic Indian Lodge. The thirty-nine-room white adobe lodge was built by the CCC and is visible from many of the trails throughout the park. At 2,700 acres, the park is fairly small (a bit smaller than Bastrop State Park), but its

The view from Davis Mountain.

elevation of between five thousand and six thousand feet above sea level does provide some challenging hiking. We started with a short drive up Skyline Drive to the Skyline Drive trailhead and then hiked out to the Keesey Canyon Overlook.

It was clear even before we got out of the car that hiking in this part of the state was a world away from that in other parts of the state, like the Sam Houston National Forest. The rugged remoteness of the area was relieved by pops of green dotting the landscape. It was easy to see where water ran off or a hidden spring existed by the almost fluorescent green color of the cottonwoods in the area. The rest of the landscape was barren and stark, with a few scrubby, tan grasses barely reaching ankle height. The views went on for miles but there were almost no towns anywhere. It was about twenty miles to Marfa or Alpine to the south and forty-five miles to Balmorhea in the north, with its famed swimming hole. We continued along the Skyline Drive Trail to the King's Table.

The King's Table.

This hidden picnic site could seat fourteen comfortably and was a great place for views. We marveled at the Chihuahuan Desert landscape as we passed cacti and a herd of javelina in the distance. We scanned the horizon for bighorn sheep but came up empty. The silence of the day was impressive. With so few people around, in a place dozens of miles away from any highways, we were not used to the unusual quiet, which would be surpassed only by Big Bend Ranch State Park. From the King's Table, it was a short one-mile hike down to Fort Davis. We decided not to do this but instead drove there when we were done, given our time pressure to get to our resting spot, Terlingua, by nightfall.

After the Skyline Drive Trail, we headed over to the Indian Lodge to check it out. The white adobe structure is visible from many of the mountains surrounding it, providing a beacon to anyone who might get turned around. This CCC creation was built in the 1930s and has thirty-nine rooms. The rooms are affordable, but be sure to book far in advance. On the way out, we visited the Limpia Creek Vista via the

Left: The Indian Lodge, which opened in 1935.

Right: View from the Indian Lodge.

short Vista Trail. It gave us a stunning view of the park and cemented great memories for us. Even though our visit to Fort Davis was somewhat short, it was a place we all enjoyed, and we were already planning our next visit there.

A brewery not to miss when you are heading to or from West Texas, or even just on a day trip in the Hill Country, is the Fredericksburg Brewing Company. It is the oldest brewpub still in operation in Texas. It was founded in 1994 right after Texas passed legislation approving the operation of brewpubs. Located on Main Street in the charming German-settled town of Fredericksburg, the large restaurant has a main room where you can sip your brew, or you can go out in the biergarten or even walk along the street, where open containers are allowed. The brewery is in a building dating back to the 1890s and sports flags from around the world, and most importantly, we noticed, from Texas A&M University!

Tom and Lou experiencing awe at the vastness of the Davis Mountains.

Did you know?

BEER IN TEN LANGUAGES BESIDES ENGLISH

Sitting in a German biergarten, we wondered how to say "beer" in different languages:

- ★ Bia—Swahili
- ★ Bier—German
- ★ Bière—French
- ★ Bira—Turkish
- ★ Birra—Italian
- ★ Cerveza—Spanish
- ★ Olut—Finnish
- ★ Pia—Maori
- ★ Serbesa—Filipino
- ★ 啤酒—Mandarin (simplified), pronounced "pijo"

We were there on a beautiful Sunday afternoon, and visitors were strolling the streets and ducking in and out of the shops and restaurants on Main Street. We got seats at the bar and ordered our first beers. They had seven beers on tap that day. Their four staples are a porter, a blonde, a red ale, and a pale ale, and the other taps rotate regularly. Deb started with the smooth Honey Cream Ale, and Jay ordered the American-style Harper Valley IPA. The Cream Ale had just the right amount of sweetness coming through from the local honey mixed in during the brewing process. We couldn't leave without trying some of the food, so Deb ordered tasty beef sliders, and Jay chose the filling sausage sampler. The menu offered everything from typical German fare like sausages and pretzels to pizza and chicken-fried steak. To go with lunch, Deb's next beer selection was El Hefe. She can't drink at a German establishment without trying a Hefeweizen. This was a classic and went nicely with the sliders.

Left: The bar at Fredericksburg Brewing Company, Fredericksburg.

Below: Our favorite Texas universities.

A Honey Cream Ale and a Harper Valley IPA at the oldest brewpub in Texas.

It was fun to be in this bustling historic brewpub, sitting directly in front of the large copper and stainless-steel tanks and watching the brewers do their brewing. The brewing company calls itself "Your Brewery," and we really did feel like we tapped into something that belongs to everyone.

The great emptiness of Big Bend Ranch State Park.

24

THE SOUND OF SILENCE

Just the facts

- ★ **HIKE:** Big Bend Ranch State Park, Contrabando Multi-Use Trail System
- ★ **BREWERY:** Jester King Brewery, Austin
- ★ **DATE:** April 16
- ★ **LENGTH:** Around 9 miles
- ★ **TYPE:** Out-and-back with some side trails
- ★ **RESTROOMS:** Just at the visitor station
- ★ **TIME:** 3:33
- ★ **STEPS:** 18,155
- ★ **RAMBLERS:** Jay, Deb, Lou, and Tom

On this day we were going off the beaten path, to Big Bend's little sister, Big Bend Ranch State Park. This park covers over three hundred thousand acres and has 238 miles of multiuse trails, so the claim to be anyone's little sister may be a misnomer. This is the biggest park in the Texas state park system and truly conveys the vastness of the Big Bend region. The drive from the Barton Warnock Visitor Center on the east side of the park to the Fort Leaton State Historic Site on the western side is forty-seven miles. Dallas, with its 1.3 million Texans, would fit nicely in the park with room to spare. Big Bend Ranch State Park is immense and empty.

Driving in from Terlingua, where we were staying, we stopped at the Barton Warnock Visitor Center to use the only nearby restroom, grabbed a map, and plotted our route with the park rangers. They recommended the Contrabando Multi-Use Trail System, with twenty-five miles of old wagon trails traversing the desert. This sounded like a good plan as we headed into the park. To the left was a swatch of green outlining the banks of the Rio Grande, which forms the southern border of the park. As we entered the parking lot by the West Trailhead, we were the lone car in the lot. We had also been the only people at the visitor center.

Unlike Big Bend National Park, this area has a feeling of isolation and desolation, and we understand now why it is called "Contrabando." Historically, the remoteness and vastness of the area made it the perfect place for smuggling goods into the United States. The feeling of being in a Cormac McCarthy novel is palpable, but the desert is also beautiful. We followed the trail while lizards scurried out of our path. Desert flowers bloomed in the most unlikely places. We were on the trail by 9:15 a.m. before the heat of the day had set in and could appreciate the beauty of the scene.

Desert blooms along the Contrabando Trail.

Jay, Tom, and Lou enjoying the "sound of silence."

After about an hour of hiking, two cyclists passed us on the trail. Although we didn't know it at the time, these would be the only two people we would see during our three-and-a-half-hour journey. After hiking for around two hours, we needed a break. Sitting on the side of the mountain, gazing at the vast land surrounding us, we fell into a quiet meditative trance. According to acoustic ecologist Gordon Hempton, author of *One Square Inch of Silence*, there are only twelve places left in the United States where you can't hear sounds made by humans. While he lists only two of these, I am pretty sure we found a third. The quiet of the area enveloped us. Not a car, airplane, or other noise could be heard, just the desert breeze crossing the barren landscape. Sadly, the one sound Jay didn't hear was his CamelBak slowly draining all its water onto the dry landscape. Deb, who had been taking pictures instead of sitting quietly, broke the sound of silence a few minutes later to explain what the "golden hour" is for photographers. She said it's the hour before sunset when the daylight is softer and redder, making for more interesting pictures. After our golden silence, we decided it must be time to head to our next destination, the Cinnabar Mine.

Did you know?

Cinnabar is a highly toxic mineral that contains mercury. It was once used in jewelry but because of its toxic nature, it no longer is. Several cinnabar mines were located in Big Bend Ranch, and stories abound of workers and mine owners suffering adverse health consequences because of the toxicity of the cinnabar.

After our Zen experience, we headed back to the trail and passed several relics of the old mines and living area. Vintage junk dotted the landscape, with broken glass smoothed by decades of shimmering in the sunlight. As we turned back toward the car, the sun had risen high in the sky and temperatures were again pushing into ninety-degree territory. Out of water, Jay began to feel like he was trudging through the desert in search of an oasis. We followed a dry riverbed on the way back with walls higher than Jay's head—indicating that an impressive stream of water had once flowed through this area. Now it was dry like the surrounding landscape. With climate change and the use of large amounts of water from the Rio Grande, this stream was unlikely to flow again outside of the occasional flash flood.

As the heat continued to intensify, we passed some old barbed wire fence that most likely demarcated the former ranchland. As Jay spotted our vehicle, alone again in the parking lot and holding several bottles of water in the trunk, he knew he had found his oasis. Day two of our Big Bend adventure had ended.

Well, the hiking had ended. Our accommodations in Terlingua were an adventure all their own. After the end of cinnabar mining, what was a booming mining town slowly became a ghost town. Now Terlingua is a popular base camp for Big Bend adventurers and is known for the original Chili Cook-off. While we could have rented a house outside the eccentric ghost town, we decided to stay in the

A dry riverbed in Big Bend Ranch State Park.

middle of it, in Lotus tents—equipped with real beds, sinks, floor rugs, and swamp coolers. Even though we had booked months ahead, there were not enough tents, so Deb took one for the team and rented an air-conditioned Airstream trailer. It was great at the end of a day of hiking to gather around a campfire with cold brews and recount our favorite sights of the day.

Tonight, we had a special treat—beers we had packed with us from our stop at Jester King Brewery on the way out. This brewery is about sixteen miles west of Austin, and you can hit it on a day-trip or on your way to Big Bend. Since breweries are few and far between in West Texas, we brought our own. Jester King is more than just a brewery—it's a destination. The 165-acre ranch houses a brewery, kitchen, farm, and event hall. This farmhouse brewery sources local agriculture, foraged plants, and native yeast. Started by two brothers, Jester King opened for business in 2010. On a stroll around the grounds, you can

Glamping in Terlingua.

Deb's even better glamping in an Airstream with air conditioning in Terlingua.

visit places like the brewhouse, the pole barn, the vineyard, and the goat barn. Dotted across the landscape are groupings of picnic tables and strings of lights.

There always seems to be live music and a feeling of celebration when you are there. Deb cracked open the OG Wytchmaker, a nice hazy rye IPA, while Jay chose Le Petit Prince, which at 2.9 percent ABV was all he could handle after a big day of hiking. Inspired by

A beer outdoors is best, especially when it's a Jester King Wytchmaker IPA.

The beautiful lawn at Jester King Brewery, Austin.

classic European farmhouse breweries, Jester King focuses on spontaneous fermentation and clean-style beers. It is known for specializing in wild, native-Texas yeast cultures in its brewing operations—kind of like getting your hiking and nature inside your beer! The beer list is unique and includes several styles brewed with fruits and herbs including grapes, watermelon, lavender, and coriander. On the way out, we stopped for some food at the brewery. While you can get traditional Texas fare like a chopped brisket or pulled pork sandwich, you can also try a wood-fired artisanal pizza. Deb loved the Pleurotus, with bechamel, mushrooms, and a balsamic reduction.

While the beer and food are showstopping, it really is the atmosphere that brings you back. Once when she was there, Deb took a walk around the ranch and loved seeing kids playing with the goats at the goat barn and groups of friends sharing stories and drinks under the twinkling lights in small groves of trees. No fooling, Jester King really is a special place that we highly recommend.

25

WHAT A WONDERFUL WORLD

Just the facts

- ★ **HIKE:** Big Bend National Park
- ★ **BREWERY:** KinderHill Brew Lab, Bryan
- ★ **DATES:** April 15 / April 17
- ★ **LENGTH:** About 10 miles each day
- ★ **TYPE:** Lots of choices—everything we did was on the east or west side
- ★ **RESTROOMS:** Yes, several, well maintained
- ★ **TIME:** 4:08 / 3:25
- ★ **STEPS:** 22,512 / 21,653
- ★ **RAMBLERS:** Jay, Deb, Lou, and Tom

This was it, our capstone. They say you can't write a book about hiking in Texas and not include Big Bend. You know what? They're right. It was everything we thought it would be and more. On the way in we drove through the infamous Marfa. We toured around town stopping by the Hotel Paisano with its walls plastered with movie memorabilia from *Giant*, which put Marfa on the map way back in 1955. From there we headed to the town of Alpine, gazing longingly at the shuttered Big Bend Brewery, which closed at the end of 2020—leaving this area almost defunct of craft beer outside of the

Brick Vault Brewery in Marathon. Sadly, our itinerary would not leave time for a visit to Marathon, but we hope to get it in on our next trip to Big Bend.

From Alpine, we headed south to our accommodations in Terlingua. Nestled between the national and state parks, this is a great place to stay for multiday hiking. The next morning, we were up at dawn ready to hike. Tom and Lou's son, David, was heading out on a long overnight bike ride through the park. After we wished him well and sent him on his way, it was time to start hiking. Grabbing the national park newsletter, "The Paisano," we planned our route. While we had originally planned several hiking routes, we needed to pivot because a wildfire had broken out in the Chisos Mountains a few days before. This closed a large area of the park, including the Chisos Mountains Lodge as well as the popular Window and Lost Mine Trails. We decided to spend the day on the west side of the park along the Ross Maxwell Scenic Drive and selected four trails to hike: the Sam Nail Ranch Trail, the Chimneys Trail, the Mule Ears Spring Trail, and Santa Elena Canyon.

After driving miles into the park to drop David off, we were a little late starting out, not hitting the Sam Nail Ranch Trail until almost 10:00 a.m. This short, half-mile hike has nice views of the remains of a ranch that once stood on the property, including a windmill. It was shady and gave us a good introduction to Big Bend. We couldn't help thinking about what it would have been like to live in such a remote location during the working days of the ranch.

Next, we headed to the Chimneys Trail. This hike was just under five miles out-and-back. Most of the hike was a walk through a desert valley. Up close, we enjoyed the life of the desert floor, with lizards and insects skirting around us. Despite the arid environment, the valley was teeming with life. In the distance, the Chimney rock formations stood out against the baby-blue sky, reminding us of how far we had to go. Finally we arrived, and the rock formations were stunning. We had a blast climbing the different features and found several

Left: Sam Nail Ranch.

Below: Chimneys Trail.

The remoteness of Big Bend.

areas where Native American pictographs were drawn. The top of the Chimneys provided a stunning view of the Chihuahuan Desert and for the first time gave us an impression of the sheer size of Big Bend National Park. At 1,252 square miles, it is bigger than Jay's home state of Rhode Island. Given all the news stories about crowds at national parks, we expected lots of people, but because of the size of the park and the numerous trails, we were by ourselves most of the time.

By the time we headed back, it was getting hot. Even in mid-April, temperatures well into the nineties in the park are not unusual. Bring plenty of water on this trail and a hat. There is literally no shade. After what seemed like a much longer way out than in, we finally arrived back at our vehicle with the sweet promise of air conditioning and lunch!

After lunch and an hour of cooling down, we were back on the trail at Mule Ears. The name of this trail makes sense as soon as you start down it and see two rock outcroppings in the distance looking pretty

Left: Santa Elena Canyon.

Right: Playing in the Rio Grande.

much like a set of mule ears. This was another out-and-back trail and was just under four miles. We headed back into the desert with the promise of a small spring at the end of the trail. This hike was a bit deceptive. "The Paisano" promised only twenty feet of elevation gain compared to the four hundred at Chimneys. Our guess is, if you go up and down and end up in the same place there is no elevation gain, but this hike was a lot hillier than Chimneys.

The views of the valley were stunning, with the trail traversing several dry arroyos along the way. The trail meandered past several old structures out in the wilderness, before finally ending at a spring. Out of nowhere, we arrived at the green oasis. The trees looked almost luminescent green as we heard the trickle of water before finding it. Surrounded by rocks and moss, a small pool of murky water was fed by a spring where both plant and animal life thrived. We were once again amazed at how life finds a way even in the starkest of conditions.

Left: Enjoying a Dos Equis in the river.
Right: Jay and Deb walking down the Rio Grande.

Finally, at 4:30 in the afternoon, we arrived at Santa Elena Canyon. Deb ran splashing into the Rio Grande, while Tom, Lou, and Jay took in the stunning vista. The cliffs on the Mexican side of the canyon rose more than 1,500 feet, providing an almost tunnel-like pathway for the river. We saw signs warning about illegal border crossings at this point, but that didn't stop Deb from wanting to wade through the water to Mexico.

We followed the short 1.6-mile out-and-back trail up and back down the US side of the canyon. Two kayakers paddled quietly down the canyon while a couple walked through the water, splashing as they went. After what seemed like way more than 0.8 miles, we ended up next to the Rio Grande. Tom, our trip planner and chief navigator, was always prepared and had brought some beers to drink while standing in the river.

Lou, our most adventurous, decided to explore some more while we enjoyed our beers. Not three minutes later, we heard her shriek and run back to us. "Snake, I saw a snake!" she yelled. That was the second and last snake we saw on our hikes. Jay never spotted one and was pretty happy about that. After all that excitement, we realized it was getting late and we needed to head back. Deb, who is more of a water person than a desert person, wanted to wade back through the river. She came prepared with her water shoes. Although Jay wasn't too excited about walking 0.8 miles barefoot through the Rio Grande, he was less excited about climbing up the trail again and decided to join her, while Tom and Lou took the smarter and drier route.

We made our way slowly through the river, leaving a muddy tail behind us. Everything was going well until Deb decided she just had to go to Mexico. As she approached the bank, it got muddier and muddier. Suddenly her water shoe was pulled right off her foot and started sinking in the mud. She shooed Jay away as he tried to help, afraid that he would get caught in the same sticky mud. This is how it ends, Jay thought, Deb swallowed by mud trying to illegally cross the border. Who would have thought? Luckily, a few harrowing minutes later, Deb freed herself and her shoe from the mud. We won't say whether she actually ever crossed into Mexico, but we did call her "La Mujer de Rio" for the rest of the night.

On our second day of hiking in Big Bend we headed to the east side of the park. This was the best hiking day we experienced in writing the whole book. From a cool misty canyon where bears play to wild horses on the beach, it was that kind of day.

We didn't have a plan for this day, unlike our normal preparation. With wildfires in the Chisos Mountains and the west-side hikes mostly completed, we planned to head to the east side of the park—but which trail to pick was still a mystery. We stopped at Panther Junction on the way in and asked the park ranger to recommend the best hike for a moderately fit, moderately experienced group of hikers. Without missing a beat, she said, "Pine Canyon Trail." We followed the rutted, winding dirt road to the trailhead. We had reserved a Jeep Wrangler back in Austin, but when we got to the rental counter, they said they didn't have any. Now, in our little Kia SUV, we were

Pine Canyon Trail.

wishing we had the Jeep. After a hair-raising and extremely bumpy thirty-minute drive, we reached the parking lot, where only a van and two other cars were parked. We headed off on a dirt track, slowly climbing through the desert. The first thing we noticed was how chilly we were. In contrast to the previous days in the blazing sun, it was now in the upper forties, with a mist covering the mountains. The trail was not superlong, just 4.3 miles out-and-back, but it did have some elevation gains near the end that made it a bit challenging.

The trail provided great views of the Chisos Mountains as we steadily climbed toward the valley. The terrain changed from upper desert scrubland into a forested wonderland. We saw a squirrel run by and wondered how the heck it got into the forest when there were hundreds of miles of desert surrounding us. It turns out that the squirrels have been here since the last ice age, much like the maples in Lost Maples State Natural Area. This was not the case for the black bears. They had been wiped out of the area by the time Big Bend became a national park back in the 1940s. Since the 1980s, people have

Majestic views of the Chisos Mountains while climbing the Pine Canyon Trail.

been spotting bears that migrated across the Rio Grande from Mexico. Today there are thirty to forty bears in the park, and this was one of their favorite areas.

Did you know?

ICE AGE

No, we're not talking about the great freeze of 2021, but rather the epoch that ended about ten thousand years ago. While Texas was not under the ice sheet, it did affect a lot of the flora and fauna. From woolly mammoths in Waco to the lost maples and squirrels in Big Bend, the effects of the ice age can still be seen today.

The trail ended in a canyon with a waterfall. On the day of our hike, it was just a trickle, but you can tell it really flows in the winter months. We ran into a bird-watching group at the end of the hike and talked to the guide, who told us about a documentary called *Big Bend: The Wild Frontier of Texas*, which had been shot there the previous year. He told us that bears would hang out right at that spot and watch them film the movie. Sadly, we didn't see any bears on our journey.

After the hike, we drove down to Rio Grande Village. As we approached the mountains, clouds poured over the range. It looked like an avalanche of snow rather than clouds. Sadly, the Boquillas Crossing was closed, so we couldn't head over to Mexico. Jay's dream of ordering *tacos con queso* in Mexico was dashed. The hot springs were also closed, so we hiked the Rio Grande Village Nature Trail.

Although this was a short 1.2-mile loop hike, it was worth it just for the breathtaking vista. This site has been occupied for thousands of years and there are mortar holes in the limestone that were used to grind grain. The gentle climb led to a wondrous view of the Rio Grande and into Mexico. There were also supposedly beavers and

Left: Canyon at the end of the trail—no bears or waterfalls spotted today.

Below: Clouds blanket the mountains in Big Bend National Park.

Rio Grande Village Nature Trail.

their dams around a water crossing, though we didn't see them. It was not looking like this was our day for animal sightings.

We decided to finish our last day by hiking Boquillas Canyon. After two days and over twenty miles of hiking, we were starting to feel it. The cool morning mist was now long gone, and temperatures were rising into the nineties again. This was a great one to finish on—the three-mile round trip brought us down into the canyon to a tributary of the Rio Grande. On the way we passed two guys who had come over from Mexico with their mules and were selling burritos by the trailside. This was one of the more popular hikes. While no trail was completely empty in Big Bend, this certainly qualified as well trafficked. We made our way down to the water and basked in the peace and quiet of the river. While the formal trail seemed to end at the water, it was easy to walk farther into the canyon. We followed a small group of people down a narrower trail. With every step, there were fewer and fewer hikers around us, until the trail ended on a small beach and we were rewarded with a band of wild horses drinking and foraging

Left: We spotted wild horses in Boquillas Canyon.
Right: Boquillas Canyon.

by the riverside. Finally, after not finding bears and beavers, we had seen our mammals for the day. We smiled giddily with excitement. If this wasn't the best way to complete our hikes, we don't know what was. It was another example of the mystery, majesty, and splendor of wild Texas. While this ended our journey and the Texas summer was rapidly approaching, we were heading home and already thinking about where we would hike next.

The Big Bend Brewery was closed, so back in Terlingua we had to make do with brews from other parts of the state and nearby. At the famous Starlight Theatre, we weren't getting much other than a Lone Star or Corona. New Texas and Old Texas. Appropriate. And sometimes a Lone Star is all you need. At our favorite Terlingua watering hole, the High Sierra Bar and Grill, Deb and Tom got cans of Local Buzz, a honey rye golden ale from the Four Corners Brewing Company in Dallas, and Jay had a can of Happy Camper, an IPA from Santa Fe Brewing Company. The night we were dining and drinking at High

Outdoor space at KinderHill Brew Lab, Bryan.

Sierra, an eccentric local band played, with a lead singer called Dr. Fun. Their song "Ghostland" sticks with us still today. One of the band members, Patrick Smith, left us with this notable quote, "Other places lift your spirit. This place lifts your soul." So true.

As we headed back to Aggieland, we decided to meet at a brewery to reminisce about the trip and all the adventures we had been on. Opened in May 2021, the KinderHill Brew Lab is a welcome addition to the beer scene in Bryan–College Station. Owners Jason and Laura bring the art and science of brewing together in their new establishment with a nice mix of unique beers. The best part of the brewery, though, is the setting. The biergarten is a large open lawn with tree shade, trellises, twinkling lights, lots of tables, and lawn games. It is one of the few places in town where you can gather and sip drinks with pets and friends and kids in an expansive, comfortable outdoor space. It is also conveniently located near Historic Downtown Bryan.

You can order your beers inside in the cozy tasting room or outside at a bar on one edge of the lawn. The outside bar offers KinderHill

A beautiful ending—nightfall in the outdoor space at KinderHill Brew Lab.

brews, a few guest beers, and a creative selection of house-made cocktails. The food scene includes a rotation of food trucks parked behind the outside bar. One night the food truck offered burgers and fries, and other times it has been tacos or even the food truck from our local eatery, Napa Flats.

On our visit to the brewery, Deb ordered the Stratusfaction hazy IPA. It was smooth and very satisfying! Jay tried the Nightmare Irish dry stout with a hint of chocolate. Next, Jay sampled the Dripping with Blood (Orange), a milkshake IPA, and Deb had the Powered by Pink with hints of hibiscus. All the tasty beers reflected the pride of the owners in their craft.

On the chilly night when we were having a beer with some mutual friends, we looked across at the twinkling lights and heard laughter from tables near us. We were reminded once again that whether you are out on the trails soaking in all the grandness nature has to offer, or sitting around a small table with friends enjoying the simple pleasure of a beer—really, what a wonderful world.

Cheers!

APPENDIX

All routes were calculated using Google Maps from the Jack K. Williams Administration Building on the Texas A&M University campus.

Hikes	Miles from Aggieland
Lake Somerville State Park	34
Little Lake Creek Trail	46
Huntsville State Park	61
Lone Star Trail, Trailhead #6	75
Bastrop State Park	76
Granger Lake	77
Buescher State Park	78
Stephen F. Austin State Park	80
Double Lake Trail	81
Mother Neff State Park	99
McKinney Falls State Park	107
Barton Springs Greenbelt	107
Bull Creek Greenbelt	109
River Place Nature Trail	115
Brazos Bend State Park	115
Inks Lake State Park	145
Pedernales Falls State Park	146
Sea Rim State Park	200
Lost Maples State Natural Area	246
Garner State Park	263
Davis Mountains State Park	530
Big Bend National Park	540
Big Bend Ranch State Park	625

Brews	**Miles from Aggieland**
KinderHill Brew Lab	5
Blackwater Draw Brewing Company	6
Brazos Valley Brewing Company	40
Lone Pint Brewery	56
B52 Brewing Company	58
Southern Star Brewing Company	64
Copperhead Brewery	67
Iron Bridge Icehouse	78
602 Brewing Company	78
Bare Arms Brewing	91
Braman Winery and Brewery	92
Buffalo Bayou Brewing Company	93
Rentsch Brewery	97
Live Oak Brewing Company	102
Lazarus Brewing Company	104
Austin Beerworks	105
Austin Beer Garden and Brewing Company	107
Hold Out Brewing	114
Jester King Brewery	122
Vista Brewing	130
Save the World Brewing Company	143
Buckstin Brewing	172
Blue Star Brewing Company	179
Fredericksburg Brewing Company	182
Pint and Plow Brewing Company	205

GLOSSARY OF TERMS

ABV—Alcohol by volume, how much alcohol a beer contains.

barley wine—A high-alcohol beer with complex flavors. To make barley wine, the brewer uses a lot more barley and, to balance the sweetness, more hops.

blazes—Trail markers, usually on trees, to show which way the trail goes.

bottom-fermenting beer—A beer in which the yeast ferments at the bottom of the brew, usually for a longer time, leading to a crisp taste typically found in lagers.

CCC—Civilian Conservation Corps, a voluntary work program that ran from 1933 to 1942 for young, unemployed, single men that created many of the structures still standing in state parks today.

cinnabar—A highly toxic mineral that contains mercury.

craft beer—Beer from a small, independent brewer.

El Camino Real de Los Tejas—A 2,500-mile trail that runs from Mexico to Louisiana. A former trade and military route, it is marked throughout much of Central Texas.

flight of beer—A small tasting of a variety of different beers.

German Reinheitsgebot—Purity law requiring that beer be made with only four ingredients: malt, hops, yeast, and water.

Hefeweizen—A beer brewed with traditional Bavarian wheat; has a cloudy appearance, high carbonation, and flavors of banana and clove.

helles—A German-style lager beer that is bright pale yellow. It should be a bit sweet with just a hint of bitterness.

IBU—International bitterness units, a measure of how bitter a beer is. Usually driven by the amount of hops.

IPA—India pale ale, originally brewed by the British to stay fresh during the long voyage to India. Characterized by a large amount of hops.

Kölsch—A top-fermenting pale ale originating in Cologne, Germany.

lollipop hike—A hike that starts down a single trail, does a loop, and comes back on the original trail.

Märzen—A German-style lager typically served at Octoberfest.

porter—A style of beer developed in the 1700s in England, featuring dark malt and a top-fermenting yeast.

prehydration—Drinking fluid before an event to reduce the risk of dehydration and improve performance.

primitive campsite—Very basic campsite without electricity or water hook-ups. May have a composting toilet nearby.

SMaSH IPA—Single malt and single hop India pale ale. Straightforward beer that allows the drinker to focus on the flavor of the malt and the hop.

stout—A style of beer similar to a porter but using unmalted roasted barley instead of malted. Traditionally it was a strong porter known as a stout porter.

top-fermenting beer—A beer in which the yeast ferments at the top of the brew, usually in less time and at a higher temperature, leading to a more favorable concoction.

trailhead—The starting point of a trail.

zythophile—A person who loves beer.

FOR MORE INFORMATION

We consulted a lot of reference material while writing this book. Some of our favorite sources are listed here. We also consulted all the brewery websites, which are not listed but provide useful information along with operating hours, food offerings, and current beers on tap.

AllTrails—This great app provides trail recommendations and lets you follow along on your route. While we use this one, there are many to choose from in the Apple App and Google Play stores. https://www.alltrails.com/

Beer Connoisseur—This is an excellent site to get educated about everything to do with beer. The education tab discusses different beer styles and trends in the industry. https://beerconnoisseur.com/

Craft Beer and Brewing—This site explains the brewing industry and features an informative podcast and newsletter. https://beerandbrewing.com/

Hop Culture—This clever site highlights things like beer travel, gear, and the creators' favorite beers throughout the year. https://www.hopculture.com/

National Park Service—While we have only two national parks in Texas (Big Bend and Guadalupe Mountains), there are actually fourteen sites in Texas run by the National Park Service. These include national monuments, recreation areas, preserves, historic trails, memorials, and historic sites. https://www.nps.gov/index.htm

Texas Craft Brewers Guild—While this is mostly a trade association, it does have a nice map of breweries around the state if you're looking for a new brewery. https://texascraftbrewersguild.org/directory-brewery-members/#!directory/map

Texas Hiking—This detailed site provides a searchable database of hikes all across Texas. http://www.texashiking.com/

Texas Parks and Wildlife—This site provides more information about different types of hikes across the state. https://tpwd.texas.gov/state-parks/parks/things-to-do/hiking-in-state-parks

Texas State Historical Association—Organized way back in 1897, this organization provides a plethora of resources on the history of Texas. https://www.tshaonline.org/home

Texas State Parks—This is the place to find state parks, make reservations, download maps, and find out everything you need to know about our state park system. https://tpwd.texas.gov/state-parks/

Untappd—This is the definitive craft beer app. Many breweries use this to keep their beer menus updated. Individuals can check in and rate the beers they drink. This is a fun way to connect with other craft beer connoisseurs. https://untappd.com/

INDEX